THE
PENDLETON
DISASTER
OFF CAPE COD

THE
PENDLETON
DISASTER
OFF CAPE COD

THE GREATEST SMALL BOAT RESCUE
IN COAST GUARD HISTORY

A True Story

THERESA MITCHELL BARBO, JOHN GALLUZZO
AND CAPTAIN W. RUSSELL WEBSTER, USCG (RET.)

Charleston London

History
PRESS

Published by The History Press
Charleston, SC 29403
www.historypress.net

Front cover: On February 20, 1952, two days after a nor'easter snapped the T-2 tanker *Pendleton* in two, Richard Kelsey photographed the hulk off Chatham, Cape Cod. CG Station Chatham's cook, Fred Wahrenburger, and another crewman look on.
Back cover: The *36500* Gold Medal crew outside Station Chatham in May 2002. *Courtesy of Bernard C. Webber.*

First published 2007

Manufactured in the United Kingdom

ISBN 978.1.59629.248.2

Library of Congress Cataloging-in-Publication Data

Barbo, Theresa M.
The Pendleton disaster off Cape Cod : the greatest small boat rescue in Coast Guard history / Theresa Barbo, John Galluzzo, and W. Russell Webster.
    p. cm.
 ISBN 978-1-59629-248-2 (alk. paper)
1. Pendleton (Tanker)--History. 2. CG36500 (Lifeboat)--History. 3. Shipwrecks--Massachusetts--Chatham-
-History. 4. Survival after airplane accidents, shipwrecks, etc.--History. I. Galluzzo, John. II. Webster, W.
Russell. III. Title.
 G530.P418B37 2007
 910.9163'46--dc22

                                    2007011827

For my son,
Thomas Daniel Barbo
—Theresa M. Barbo

I would like to dedicate this book to every Coast Guardsman I have ever met,
and to those of whom I have not had the pleasure.
—John Galluzzo

To my heroes—Bernie, Andy, Ervin and Richard
— Captain W. Russell Webster, USCG (Ret.)

Contents

Acknowledgements

An immense debt of thanks to the crew of the *36500*, to Bernie, Andy, Richard and to the memory of the late Ervin, as well as Charles Bridges who served on the *Pendleton*, who patiently sat for my interviews in the parlor of Mariners' House in Boston in May 2002. To Miriam Webber, always cheerful and lovely, I give my thanks for simply being there through the years.

A debt of thanks to Captain W. Russell Webster, USCG (Ret.), and to John J. Galluzzo of Weymouth, both of whom complemented this project, and for their contributions. Most of all, I thank my children, Katherine and Thomas, and my husband, Dan.

Theresa Mitchell Barbo
Yarmouth Port, Cape Cod, Massachusetts

I would like to thank Captain W. Russell Webster, USCG (Ret.), for his dedication to the ongoing quest to assure that the Coast Guardsmen of America are not forgotten for what they do and have done. To the many members of the U.S. Life-Saving Service Heritage Association for their help and support over the years, especially Commander Maurice Gibbs USN (Retired) of Nantucket; Richard Boonisar of South Dennis, Massachusetts; Fred Stonehouse of Marquette, Michigan; Ralph Shanks of Novato, California; Dennis L. Noble of Sequim, Washington; and many, many more. My thanks to BMCS David Considine, USCG, for keeping the history of the Coast Guard in Chatham alive and well; William D. Wilkinson of Springfield, Pennsylvania, and Tim Dring of Robinsville,

Acknowledgements

New Jersey, for their expertise on the history of lifeboats, both motorized and shoulder-powered; LCDR Fred "Bud" Cooney, USCGR (Retired) of Charlestown, Rhode Island, for remembering where he was on February 18, 1952, and sharing his story; Dick Ryder and Pete Kennedy and the rest of the Orleans History Society, today's guardians of the CG *36500*; and all of the members of today's U.S. Coast Guard for protecting our shores and our lives when we are on the sea.

John Galluzzo
Hull, Massachusetts

To my wife, Elizabeth, and children, Andrew and Noelle: for their patience and understanding when I became immersed in my passion for telling and writing Coast Guard stories. To authors Barbo and Galluzzo for their support of the Coast Guard's heroes, past and present.

To the Coast Guard's heroes—that one day all your stories may be told.

Captain W. Russell Webster, USCG (Ret.)

FOREWORD

By Captain W. Russell Webster, USCG (Ret.)

I first heard about the heroic 1952 rescue of thirty-two *Pendleton* crewmen in 1998 after becoming the Coast Guard's Group Woods Hole rescue commander responsible for the small multi-mission Coast Guard stations from Cape Cod to Newport.

Master Chief Boatswain Mate Jack Downey, then officer-in-charge, invited me to the Chatham Coast Guard Station to witness a ceremonial "pinning" of new chief petty officers, which to this day remains an indelible personal memory.

"Pinning" involves the ceremonial "mixing" of collar devices from seasoned chief petty officers with a new set of pins for the new chief in an overturned combination cap. The concept was that the experience and ideas of the new generation were symbolically melded with their predecessors.

It all made sense, except for the one extra set of devices given out that day. The master chief explained that the extra set of chief petty officer (BMC-CPO) devices, worn smooth with time, belonged to the coxswain of the thirty-six-foot rescue craft (then) Bosun's Mate First Class (BM1) Bernie Webber—the inspiration for the tradition. His collar devices would go to the newest chief petty officer.

Downey clarified that today's generations of guardsmen are truly "standing on their [*CG36500* rescue crews'] shoulders" when they don the treasured devices of the man from a bygone era. To date, nineteen new chief petty officers have worn Webber's CPO pins and carried on a tradition of respect that will likely perpetuate for generations to come.

In the following years, I learned that there was more to the *Pendleton* rescue than met the eye: more heroics on many levels, and more pain than there should have been for the four brave crewmen, especially BM1 Webber.

The Pendleton Disaster off Cape Cod does justice to the *Pendleton* rescue story and the brave men of *CG36500* that might not have been properly told were it not for the determined efforts of my two co-authors, especially Barbo.

Pinning ceremony of MMC William Turner at Station Chatham on May 31, 1987. *Courtesy of Bernard C. Webber.*

Bernie Webber addressing the crew at Station Chatham on May 31, 1987. *Courtesy of Bernard C. Webber.*

Uncovered were memories of an unkind rescue-era Coast Guard officer corps that secretly admonished the public adulations that had been heaped on these four enlisted men the burden of leadership and haunting memories Coxswain Webber has endured for more than fifty-five years and the secret of *Pendleton* crewman Tiny Myers's death during the rescue.

You are invited to see why generations of guardsmen will always stand on the shoulders of the heroic *Pendleton* rescue crew.

INTRODUCTION

BY THERESA MITCHELL BARBO

To understand the complexity of the Coast Guard rescue effort of that night in 1952, and to absorb the full context of this uniquely personal story, please digest this introduction before you read the chapters of *The Pendleton Disaster off Cape Cod*.

On February 18, 1952, a nor'easter tore through the upper coast of the Atlantic seaboard. A nor'easter is so named for its northeast-borne winds that hit coastal areas. Meteorologists call nor'easters "macro-storms," and with justification. This particular nor'easter boasted 70-knot winds and 60-foot seas that snapped two 520-foot T-2 tankers—the SS *Fort Mercer* and SS *Pendleton*—in half, east of Cape Cod, about sixty miles apart from one another.

The *Pendleton*, registered in Baton Rouge, Louisiana, carried heating oil and kerosene and was bound for Boston. The *Fort Mercer*, destined for Portland, Maine, also carried kerosene. The *Fort Mercer* issued an SOS, but all radio contact was lost with the *Pendleton* before she could issue an alert to the Coast Guard. Those aboard waited eight hours before the ship was discovered—by accidental means—but immediately the Coast Guard responded.

The Coast Guard knew about the *Fort Mercer* way before the *Pendleton*, thanks to the *Mercer*'s SOS. The latter was discovered by a survey flight from Air Station Salem, whose pilot was actually looking for the *Fort Mercer*, but instead found the *Pendleton*.

Unbelievably, the Coast Guard now had two identical disasters to manage, and both in conditions of a ferocious nor'easter. Launched were nearly every type of rescue vessel in the Portland–, Boston– and Cape Cod–area contingents: the cutters *Eastwind*, *Unimak*, *Acushnet*, *Yakutat* and *McCulloch*. Three thirty-six-foot motor lifeboats from Cape Cod—the *36500* and *36383*—and from Nantucket, the *36524*, skippered by Chief Ralph Orsmby, BM1 Alfred J. Roy, Engineman First Class (EN1) John F. Dunn and Seaman Donald E. Pitts. Air support, additional craft and officers and seamen answered the official call to help that February night.

The SS *Pendleton. Courtesy of Bernard C. Webber.*

There was much distance between the two ships, particularly in this storm. The *Fort Mercer* was farther to sea during the storm, a good many miles, so the Coast Guard dispatched its larger cutters to reach her, including the *CG36383*. Thirty-eight merchant seamen were rescued from the *Mercer*'s stern section. Five crewmen aboard the *Mercer* were trapped in the bow and their remains were never recovered.

ENS Benedict L. Stabile, a 1950 graduate of the U.S. Coast Guard Academy, and later a vice admiral, was aboard the *Unimak* that night early into his Coast Guard career. After February 18, 1952, Stabile wrote, "I remember arriving at the scene of the *Fort Mercer* stern. We had no knowledge of the *Pendleton* disaster at the time. *Acushnet* was also on scene and there were radios comms [communications]. With the personnel on the stern section headed by the Engineer as I recall. I think a walkie talkie was passed over to the survivors." With so many Coast Guard vessels at sea attempting to rescue people in the worst possible weather conditions, many stories were underway at once.

Although this is the story of Bernie Webber, the *36500* and the rescue of the *Pendleton* crew, the rescue of the merchant seamen aboard the *Fort Mercer* proved almost as equally harrowing and heroic. According to Stabile,

> Eastwind *first tried running a rubber boat back and forth with lines between* Fort Mercer *and* Eastwind*. They managed to recover a few men that way* [three] *but the men had to clamber* [sic] *aboard* Eastwind *cargo nets. The ship, being an icebreaker,*

rolled very heavily so the men were getting the Coney Island cyclone ride with part of the cycle under water before shooting 60 feet into the air hanging on for dear life.

The *Eastwind* was commanded by Captain O.A. Peterson. Stabile added the seamen aboard the *Fort Mercer* decided to take their chances remaining on the hulk, rather than risk death on a Coney Island Cyclone ride.

Bernie Webber would be the first Coastie to say excellent seamanship did not belong only to him that night. According to Stabile, "The *Acushnet* CO then decided to take some bold steps by swinging his cutter in sharply and placing his fantail at the most convenient point for survivors to jump down to it, timing the waves for minimum distance. More than one pass was made each time several men jumped aboard successfully but then there was a nucleus that felt even that was too risky."

Stabile said the seamanship was the finest he had ever seen. "How the CO managed to execute without damaging the ship or losing anyone is beyond me." That CO of the *Acushnet*, Lieutenant Commander John M. Joseph, allowed the vessel to drift toward the *Fort Mercer* near enough to let the men jump. Most did, but a few opted to stay aboard the vessel.

Less than twenty minutes before the bow capsized, the *Yakutat* rescued the remaining four men from the *Fort Mercer* bow.

The *Unimak* had launched a lifeboat but almost lost it in the high seas. "The idea was to pick up anyone who might wind up in the water during the rescue ops and perhaps to see if there were any persons or bodies out there," wrote Stabile. "It was the roughest seas I've ever seen a boat launched in."

The stern of the *Fort Mercer* was towed to port. "We were directed to stay with the *Fort Mercer* bow until the owners and insurers decided what they wanted done with the bow, which was loaded with kerosene," Stabile said. The night passed on, and keeping track of the bow via radar proved tough. Finally, word came down to sink the bow. "I was gunnery Officer. We tried 5"/38 and 40mm HEI shells but all we did was make holes above water from which steams of kerosene spewed," Stabile recounted in a letter. With the main tanks submerged, and effects of the ordnance questionable, Stabile was worried it would take days before the bow would sink. "The skipper Cdr. Frank McCabe then directed me to use the K guns which we had never fired except for a test after installation with dummy charges. We set up the starboard side, three charges set for minimum 50 feet and McCabe wound up the engines for a max speed run hoping we would avoid damage to ourselves," Stabile remembered. Known as "Eighteen-knot McCabe," the *Unimak* sped by the bow as Stabile fired the K guns. Nothing much happened so McCabe ordered Stabile ready for a port side run. "Just as we got into the run the bow went vertical and then dropped down to the depths. It worked! We had managed to rupture the submerged tanks after all," wrote Stabile.

The *Unimak* then escorted the stern section of the *Fort Mercer* as she crept toward port, mostly to stave off pressure from the forward bulkhead. Afterward, the *Unimak* headed home to Boston. The stern of the *Fort Mercer* was used for the *San Jacinto*, a new tanker. That vessel broke in half off the Virginia coast in March 1964. For many years the hulk of the *Pendleton* lay where she died.

When the long rescue event finally ended, seventy of the eighty-four crewmembers aboard both tankers would be rescued from four portions of the two vessels in daring, multiple rescues by the Coast Guard.

All told, twenty-one Coast Guard officers and seamen were decorated for their actions at a ceremony in Washington, D.C., in May 1952, by Edward H. Foley, undersecretary of the treasury, and Vice Admiral Merlin O'Neill, Coast Guard commandant. Five received the Gold Lifesaving Medal. Four were awarded the Silver Lifesaving Medal and fifteen were decorated with a Commendation Medal at that ceremony, including Boatswain's Mate Third Class Antonio F. Ballerini, twenty, of East Boston, who passed away at seventy-two of lung cancer in 2004. "They were on the water for twenty-four hours," under the command of Donald Bangs explained his widow, Angela, speaking from her home in Cape Coral, Florida. "He never complained," she added. "That's the type of person he was."

Bernie stuck his neck out in 1952 by standing up for his crew's valor when it came time for the decorations.

"The one smart thing I did back then was to refuse the Gold Medal unless the others received it also," Bernie recounted, referring to his *36500* crew, while other Coast Guardsmen who served on the other 36-foot life boats were awarded the silver. "Headquarters wanted to give my crew the Silver Medal…the Officer at Headquarters was stunned and wondered if I meant it. I said, 'Yes and that's the way it had to be,'" Webber added.

This is the story of that one man, Bernie Webber, who led the Station Chatham crewmen to rescue imperiled strangers from one of those tankers, the SS *Pendleton*, in the truest and timeless traditions of the United States Coast Guard.

It is a true story of Bernie Webber, an authentically humble man who remained true to his ideals, and always and to the end, to the United States Coast Guard.

PART ONE

Chapter One

Sunday, May 12, 2002
6:00 p.m.
Mariners' House, Boston's North End

By Theresa Mitchell Barbo

Four stoic men in their august years stand on the red-tiled floor of a Boston hotel lobby, barely speaking. A fifth, Charles W. Bridges, is nearby. They stare uneasily at each other, shuffling their feet while making small talk. "We were virtually strangers," one of the men would later say. Other guests at Mariners' House that day walked right on by, not knowing the unique bond of the group.

Decades had passed since the last time Bernie Webber, Andy Fitzgerald, Ervin Maske and Richard Livesey were together. The awkwardness was not surprising.

Who were these men?

All four former Coast Guardsmen were on Cape Cod at Station Chatham the wintry night of February 18, 1952, when they carried out the greatest small boat rescue in modern Coast Guard history five miles off Chatham's notoriously treacherous shore.

Thirty-two crewmen aboard the oil tanker *Pendleton*, which had split in two during a nor'easter, had clamored aboard the *36500*, a thirty-six-foot lifeboat powered only by a ninety-horsepower engine. Charles Bridges was one of them. Another *Pendleton* crewman had died in the attempt.

Bernie was twenty-four and a boatswain's mate, first class. Richard was a twenty-two-year-old seaman, as was Ervin, twenty-three. Andy was the youngest, at twenty-one, an engineman, second class. For their actions the night of February 18, all received the Coast Guard's highest honor, the Gold Lifesaving Medal.

In its day the story was big news, splattered across newspapers everywhere. Within the halls of the Coast Guard, the *Pendleton* and *Fort Mercer* missions are sacrosanct, with the valiant *36500* mission remaining the greatest motor lifeboat rescue during peacetime in Coast Guard history. The rescue by the *36500* crew is a feat without equal today.

For the first time in fifty years these four men were together again in the same room, gathered by the Coast Guard—in particular by a history-minded captain—for a three-day reunion. With them was a man they had rescued off the *Pendleton*, Charles Bridges. The first leg of their reunion weekend occurred in the lobby of Mariners' House in Boston's historic North End.

In May 2002, Captain W. Russell Webster was chief of operations for First District Coast Guard in Boston, and it was he who dreamed up the goal of reuniting the *36500* rescue team. I assisted Captain Webster as chair of the committee that planned the Chatham portion of the reunion.

"These were my heroes, my idols, men who had done incredible death-defying feats in the face of incredible pain and suffering with far less training and equipment than their modern counterparts," said Captain Webster, who spent months of his own time planning the reunion. Captain Webster had long heard and read about the night the crew of the mortally wounded oil tanker, the *Pendleton*, was rescued five miles south of Chatham off Cape Cod, and planned a reunion around the Coast Guard crew. "The Coast Guard had opted to forget them for almost a half-century and it would have been easier for some of them to remain anonymous and not open old wounds and memories," he added.

With Captain Webster at the helm of the conversation, handshakes began and camaraderie renewed. Slowly, talk tricked among the small group, and feet no longer shuffled in discomfort. The years melted and the awkwardness faded.

"Oh, Ervin," was all Bernie could say, his voice cracking, when he walked forward to embrace Ervin Maske, whom he hadn't seen in fifty years, and who could barely stand following a recent operation to replace bad knees.

"He's the same Andy," Bernie would say later of Fitzgerald. "He hasn't changed one iota. He has a way about him that is as steady as can be. The only difference is his white head of hair."

"It feels pretty good to see them again," remembered Ervin. "It was worth the trip to come."

Surrounding the small circle at Mariners' House was a larger sphere of family—wives, sons, daughters, grandchildren and assorted in-laws—who had accompanied the Gold Medal Crew to Boston. Charles W. Bridges made the trip up from Florida. Charles was a young man of eighteen and a sailor aboard the 520-foot, 10,000-ton *Pendleton* the night the storm cracked the vessel in two.

Captain Webster found Bridges and brought him up for the reunion. [Aside from one other sailor too ill to attend, Bridges was the only other *Pendleton* crewman Webster's extensive search turned up.] After abandoning the stricken ship, Bridges shared the trip back to shore with the other survivors; a trip no one thought could be made, for no one expected the crew to come back alive.

Charles was keen on the trip. Although his initial connection to the Coast Guard was that of being rescued, after a two-year army stint, Bridges enlisted in the Coast Guard in 1955, and retired in 1977 as a senior chief engineer. He brought his wife, Suellen; daughter, Lorraine; and sister-in-law, Lilda, to Boston for the reunion. "It was great seeing the guys," he said from his twenty-acre farm in North Palm Beach, Florida. [Suellen Bridges passed on in 2004.]

It took some convincing by Webster to persuade Webber, who teeters on cynicism at times, that a reunion would work.

When Captain Webster approached Bernie about the reunion, Webber had understandable reservations. "Very much so, because I wasn't sure what his motivation was, what he was thinking," said Webber. "I didn't think it was a very good idea at first, but as he talked to me, he finally said to me, 'Under what conditions would you agree to it?' and I said, 'All right, let's talk about it.'"

Bernie's first question to Captain Webster was "Would such an affair be good for the Coast Guard?" Webster answered, "It would."

Bernie's first condition was that all four Gold Medal crewmembers had to attend. "If one couldn't make it, forget it," he said to Captain Webster. A second condition was that "unlike fifty years before, the families would be allowed to be present; they would be invited," and Captain Webster said yes to that request, too.

This event would have to be a Coast Guard activity, unlike, in Bernie's words, "Fifty years before when we went to Washington and not one Coast Guard officer was present, only the 'beltway types' from Washington that go to these affairs," said Bernie. Webber remembered attending an event where he felt like a puppet to promote the Coast Guard, hence the cynicism.

Captain Webster assured Bernie a reunion "wouldn't cost…money to participate in the event. Our ways would be paid," which was the fourth condition. Captain Webster agreed to all of it. After reassurance by Captain Webster, Bernie told him, "I'll try to persuade the other fellas."

Agreeing to the conditions was the easy part; now Captain Webster had to find the former Coast Guardsmen. Bernie and his wife, Miriam, had retired to Melbourne, Florida. Ervin had settled in Marinette, Wisconsin. The Coast Guard found Richard Livesey in Florida not far from Bernie, and he brought his wife, Virginia, to Boston. Andy Fitzgerald and his wife, Gloria, flew in from Colorado. A widower, Ervin Maske was accompanied by his devoted daughter, Anita Maske Jevne, and son, Matt.

Bernie himself had sporadic contact with a few crewmembers over the years. Richard Livesey phoned Bernie in Florida and visited him there once. He and Andy had exchanged a Christmas card or two.

The *Pendleton* mission, however, was a subject no man talked about. "None of us from the day of the *Pendleton* discussed any part of it."

Over the years much was written—some true, some not so true—about the *Pendleton* sinking and the story about the *36500*. Bernie had been burned numerous times, either through misquotes or negative dealings with people with a stake in the story, and was understandably leery about talking to anyone about the incident. A few tried to make money off his story. Still, he showed up in Boston to support the event and kept an eye on the other crewmen.

"I could relate to how it was fifty years previous with everybody pulling at you, tugging at you, quoting you, misquoting you, pushed here, pushed there, I didn't like it back then, and I know they didn't, and I didn't want to see a repeat of that. I thought the reunion should be a happy time, a time to do away with all the necessities of what

Bernie Webber and Captain W. Russell Webster, May 2002. *Courtesy of Theresa Mitchell Barbo.*

reporters wanted to write. I didn't know all the people who were there…so you know you want to see they're taken care of, they're treated right," he would say following the reunion.

"I was a career Coast Guardsmen, and I had known Fitzgerald and Maske had gotten out and weren't too up-to-date on how the Coast Guard deals with people, and I didn't want to see them caught up with things which made them uncomfortable," said Webber.

Therefore, five decades after their near-death at sea, Bernie's group was together again at the Mariners' House in Boston's North End.

Mariners' House, founded by a former fisherman-turned-preacher, Father Edward Thomson Tailor, is a private hotel constructed in 1847 "for the sole purpose of providing hospitality and guidance for seafarers," explained Executive Director Michael Cicalese, himself a longtime Coast Guard officer now serving in the reserves.

People from all over the world have stayed at Mariners' House. Inside are two large parlors that resemble what you would find in a Boston mansion one hundred years ago, with ample reading and gathering space. A large kitchen with cafeteria space

Left to right: Charles Bridges, Gloria Fitzgerald, Andy Fitzgerald, Virginia Livesey, Richard Livesey, Ervin Maske, Miriam and Bernie Webber. *Courtesy of Theresa Mitchell Barbo.*

and a business office are on the first floor. It is spotless inside and beautiful, due to its tall ceilings, marble floors, exquisite antique woodworking and hospitality from an accommodating staff.

Mariners' House still serves seamen from merchant vessels including the Coast Guard, which has its New England headquarters within walking distance. Mariners' House is tucked into Boston's North End and many remnants of Boston's Little Italy are retained in its quaint, narrow brick-lined street near Paul Revere's home. It's an amazing place to stay—quiet, comfortable and roomy—but it's only for mariners. The North End is still that quintessential tightly knit community: the kind of neighborhood where both young and old walk with no fear and with little crime around. Everyone seems to know everyone else. Since Captain Webster often stayed there, it proved the perfect site to house the reunion contingent while in Boston for a special luncheon and ceremony at Coast Guard Boston headquarters.

"It was special to have the crew of the *36500* at Mariners' House because it was built for merchant marine personnel, and what better way to show support and gratitude to those men who risked their lives to save—and did save—merchant mariners, than to have them under the merchant marine landmark roof," Cicalese lamented.

The Gold Medal Crew felt the same way about Mariners' House. Ervin opted to dine in Monday evening, which cost a guest as little as three dollars, even though the Coast Guard would have picked up the tab at a restaurant. He wanted nothing more than to enjoy a simple meal in a beautiful place and to rest his throbbing knees, so recently operated on.

Above: Rear Admiral Vivian Crea addressing the Gold Medal Crew in May 2002. *Courtesy of Theresa Mitchell Barbo.*

Left: Congressman William Delahunt at the May 2002 reunion. *Courtesy of Theresa Mitchell Barbo.*

Rear Admiral Vivian Crea handing Bernie Webber a Gold Medal Certificate as Captain Webster and Ervin Maske look on. *Courtesy of Theresa Mitchell Barbo.*

Bernie, slightly skeptical of the reunion at first, brought his reservations to Boston. He had no idea how this latest *Pendleton* event would come off, but he hoped for the best. Clearly, he felt protective about his men even though Andy, Ervin and Richard had long since left his command.

"I was 'still in charge,' and it's a funny thing, you're the coxswain of the boat, you're the captain of it, it's a natural thing, I don't know how they felt, but it was up to me to see they were taken care of," he said later.

The *36500* crew, their families and other assorted guests left Mariners' House to follow the brick-lined streets to dinner at an Italian restaurant around the corner hosted by Captain Webster, under a North End rain that would not let up for days. For three of the Gold Medal crew, it would be several days to remember.

Bernie Webber dreaded the ceremonies planned for the days ahead, and all the fuss and angst he was about to shoulder again. Would this be reminiscent of the 1950s, when the Coast Guard paraded Webber on public relations junket after junket, or had things changed enough for a less troubled series of events?

The day, Monday, the *36500* crew attended "A Luncheon to Honor Heroes," arranged by Captain Webster at the Coast Guard base in Boston. It not only was a huge event, but also a huge success. Bernie was not disappointed. An oil portrait entitled *Pendleton Rescue* by Robert Selby was unveiled. Rear Admiral Vivian Crea and Congressman William Delahunt, himself a Coast Guard veteran, were the honored guests. In prepared remarks, Admiral Crea reaffirmed the significance of that one mission in February 1952 and said she was thrilled to meet each Gold Medal crewman. "This is the stuff of which legends are made…it is the stuff that is the basic foundation of the Coast Guard, which motivates the heroes amongst us even today."

As the Coast Guard had done half a century before, Admiral Crea and Congressman Delahunt presented Bernie and his crew with reissued lifesaving medal award certificates signed by the 2002 Coast Guard Commandant Admiral James M. Loy.

Bernie listened to the speeches and watched the faces of the many Coast Guard guests who had come to honor the *36500* crew, for many accepted Captain Webster's blanket invitation. Ever so slightly, it appeared, the tide of resentment began to recede for Bernie, who felt that for the first time in fifty years the Coast Guard had recognized the entire crew for doing their jobs and had not singled out Webber as a hero.

After lunch, the Gold Medal crew relaxed in Boston before leaving for the Cape the next morning, bound for Chatham and further reunion activities planned by Captain Webster. A dinner in the Village Room at the Chatham Wayside Inn was planned for Tuesday evening.

If the Boston luncheon at the Coast Guard base was formal, dinner Tuesday evening was a mix of special guests, former and current Coast Guard officers and noncommissioned officers who traded stories and goodwill with the Gold Medal crew and their families.

Bernie's face said it all: he was sharing the evening and his memories with his wife, Miriam; their daughter Patricia and her husband, Bruce; and their daughters Leah and Hilary. This was a different Coast Guard than the one young Webber joined after his rebellious teen years.

Chapter Two

A Young Man Seeks Belonging and Purpose

By Theresa Mitchell Barbo

"Idrove him crazy," Bernie says of his father, the Reverend A. Bernard Webber, a Baptist minister.

Bernard Challen Webber was born on May 9, 1928, the youngest of four boys born to Annie Knight and A. Bernard Webber, a preacher.

A strict, pious man, Reverend Webber moved his family around until they settled in affluent Milton, Massachusetts, where by 1943 "my Dad was serving as the associate pastor at Tremont Temple Baptist Church in Boston, Massachusetts," Bernie's memoirs recall.

The family's move to the Boston suburbs coincided with World War II, and the three elder Webber boys shipped out with various branches of the armed services, leaving Bernie—a tall, lanky fifteen-year-old—at home. "Brother Paul left with the first draft and served the army's Twenty-sixth Division in Germany. Brother Bob served the U.S. Coast Guard. Brother Bill served the Army Transportation Corps and was off building the Alaskan Highway," he remembered.

By his own reckoning but without much detail, Bernie confesses that as a kid he was "easily led." Through family connections and a patron, Bernie left for boarding school, Mount Hermon Preparatory at Greenfield, Massachusetts. He was strongly advised to study for the ministry. "Of course, I was not consulted," he said. A deacon at his father's church paid the tuition, and Reverend Webber picked up the cost of incidentals, but Bernie felt out of place there, especially in his brother's hand-me-down clothes. "With limited allowance, and neither scholastically nor athletically inclined, I wasn't a prime candidate for either Mount Hermon or the ministry," he would later write.

The kids from rich families worked as waiters in the dining hall, but the scholarship students and those from poorer families worked the farm. Bernie, thin but strong, was a field hand who shoveled "dung on the farm, and also worked in the laundry." To this day, he remembers the smell: "My last class, a French class, was late, and I always smelled like a cow," Webber recalled. "The French teacher would always make note of that."

"I wasn't too happy with the setup, but I was moving along," Bernie said. That all changed when a buddy from home, Milton Anderson, smashed his father's car and ran to Mount Hermon to see Bernie. Bernie could not hide Milton in his room, "because my roommate would have squealed," so instead Bernie knew "another fella" who agreed to conceal Milton, who spent a few days on the Mount Hermon campus.

Bernie decided to quit the exclusive boarding school. One night, fed up with school and using Milton as an excuse, "We fled through the cornfields in Northfield, Mass., and went home."

The senior Webber confronted Bernie about his son's future. Bernie had heard that teenagers were being accepted at sixteen as merchant seamen. He begged to go. "I talked my father into signing for me and he was glad to do it, as I was so rebellious and such a problem," Bernie said. Once basic training was over Bernie was shipped to Panama to board the SS *Sinclaire Rubiline*, "a T2 Tanker." Coincidentally, a T2 tanker would figure prominently into Bernie's life within a few short years, but not because of his time in the merchant marine.

"From the ports of Aruba and Curacao in the Caribbean we carried gasoline to the South Pacific in support of the war effort," Bernie said. In 1946 Bernie enlisted in the Coast Guard, almost on a fluke.

"I wanted to find another berth in the merchant marine to avoid the army, as I was approaching the draft age. Since shipping in the Atlantic was slow, you could turn down two ships if you didn't like what you heard," he explained. "But the third one you had to take," which was what brought Bernie to Constitution Wharf at midday in Boston. "They shut down every noontime at the shipping center."

Bernie looked for a place to eat lunch. He strolled to Constitution Wharf, where the Coast Guard was based, and saw a sign that read, "The Coast Guard Wants You." Bernie knew the Guard issued seaman's papers so in he went. There a second-class petty officer sat "with his feet up on the desk eating his lunch" and said, "What the hell do you want?"

Bernie said he saw the sign outside.

"What the hell do you have to offer the Coast Guard?"

The sign outside, Bernie mentioned.

"Well, that doesn't necessarily mean you!"

"I'm a merchant seaman," Webber replied.

"The minute I said that he perked up, took his feet off the desk and told me to sit down," Webber later recalled.

The enlistment papers required his father's signature and once Webber's father signed them, Bernie said, "Here we go again," and off to Curtis Bay, Maryland, he went for basic training.

Webber's first assignment after leaving Maryland was as a keeper of Highland Lighthouse at North Truro. Six months later, Bernie was transferred to the Gay Head

Lighthouse on Martha's Vineyard. He spent a few days at Station Chatham before leaving for the Vineyard. "I would get to know the Town of Chatham, become acquainted with the lifeboat station, and make some personal decisions about my future," he wrote. "I felt an attraction to Chatham…and sensed there was a reason I had been brought to this place."

When Bernie was driven by Old Harbor, he got his first glance at the *36500*. "At the time I wasn't particularly impressed," he said.

Station Chatham was as unique as Chatham itself. A lighthouse was in the front yard. There used to be two, hence the nickname "Twin Lights of Chatham," but one light was moved to Eastham and renamed Nauset Light. "The station equipment was spread out all around the town, necessary due to the geographic arrangement of the town and surrounding waters," Bernie said.

"One lifeboat was kept on a mooring out in Old Harbor. The other lifeboat and the picket boat were kept on the moorings at Stage Harbor. This was done so that access to the Atlantic Ocean and Nantucket Sound would be readily available under all circumstances," Webber added.

Bernie spent three years at the Gay Head Lighthouse and did a stint aboard a Coast Guard cutter in the North Atlantic.

Chatham then was not what Chatham is now, with swanky shops and a high tax base. The town revolved around its fishing piers, and that's the Chatham Bernie found when he returned in 1950 for a two-year tour at Station Chatham.

As Bernie remembers Chatham then:

> *Perhaps there was a new shop or two on Main Street, or a few more fishermen working from the Fish Pier, departing out of Aunt Lydia's Cove, crossing Chatham Bars daily in pursuit of fresh fish. Alton Kenney's boatyard was busy where he and Elisha Bearse took care of the ills of the fleet. The Sou'wester and Jake's remained as places for blowing off steam. The Dutch Oven on Main Street was available for those who wanted good coffee and conversation.*

Bernie's first rescue at Station Chatham was helping with the stranding of the USS *Livermore* in 1949. The vessel carried mostly navy reservists and stranded in a calm sea under a full moon. "For some reason when passing *Stonehorse* Lightship she did not make the necessary course change to the right which would take the ship safely up the Pollock Rip Channel passing between the buoys with their lights flashing," Bernie recalled. "Instead, the *Livermore* moved straight ahead and eventually came to a halt," resting on Bearses' Shoal off Monomoy.

Leo Gracie, a boatswain mate first class, whom Bernie respected, picked Webber to go with him, and reaching the *Livermore*, Gracie and his crew waited for larger vessels such as tugs and navy salvage ships from the Boston naval shipyard to arrive to help. Station Chatham's picket boat towed hawsers across the water several times, and transported supplies and personnel between the vessels, until the *Livermore* was free and clear.

Several more assignments landed on Bernie's lap before he was qualified to operate rescue boats, his chief goal, and subsequently go out on the *Pendleton* rescue.

Mrs. Bernard C. Webber—the former Miriam Pentinen of Wellfleet—a year after their marriage. *Courtesy of Bernard C. Webber.*

Bernie and Miriam on their wedding day, July 16, 1950, in Milton, Massachusetts. *Courtesy of Bernard C. Webber.*

As a coxswain Bernie supervised the Loran unit—a monitoring facility—at Station Chatham, then soon after, he went to the Monomoy Point Lookout Station. Then, finally, the transfer to Station Chatham came through.

Bernie's boss was the kindly Alvin E. Newcomb, a chief warrant officer with thirty years' service. Webber loved the guy. "We affectionately referred to him as 'Mother Newcomb' for several reasons. His only child was his daughter, Evelyn. As a result his crew at the station became adopted sons." Newcomb did not care for trouble among his boys: "At night Alvin Newcomb would make bed checks on his crew and roam the station yard with a flashlight in hand. Smoking the pipe that was forever in his mouth, his presence was announced long before his arrival," Bernie would later write.

"I think he planned it that way so as not to catch any of the crew that might be lurking around the station yard, in the dark, with some of the local girls."

Bernie himself was courting a local girl. Miriam Pentinen was a Wellfleet girl, born and bred on Cross Street, and daughter of Finnish immigrants Olga and Otto Pentinen She had met Bernie on a blind date, and they went to Bob Murray's Drugstore on Main Street in Wellfleet. Bernie drove his 1939 two-door Plymouth sedan. "We left the drugstore and went to a place called Ma Downer's out in South Wellfleet," Bernie would write years later. "There wasn't any place else to go in those days as they rolled the sidewalks up in the Town of Wellfleet at seven p.m. Ma Downer's was just a shack, a small place where one could sit and have a cup of coffee or drink a beer." Bernie said the date was not terribly exciting for any of them, including the other couple on the double date. "We just sat around talking and carved out initials on the wooden table."

Bernie, however, grew smitten when he and Miriam kissed and, Bernie remembered, "Bells began to ring in my head." Miriam and Bernie dated through the winter of 1950. An engagement came several months later. They married at the home of Bernie's parents, the Reverend A. Bernard and Annie Knight Webber, on July 16. "It was strange to have my father officiate, and was even somewhat more awkward for Miriam as she knew the minister would now be her father-in-law," Bernie recounted.

Bernie's marriage to Miriam grounded the young Coast Guardsman, whose formative years were challenging to his strict father, a Baptist minister. "Once married to Miriam I also felt truly united with Cape Cod," Bernie recounted in his memoirs, published in 1985. "At first we took up residence in a little upstairs apartment located in a building next door to the curtain factory in Wellfleet. I was by myself most of the time," Miriam recalls, since her new husband pulled many ten-day stints at the Chatham Station. The Webbers moved to Chatham and rented a nine-room house called Silver Heels.

It was, Miriam recalls, "nothing elaborate," but the living and dining rooms were comfortable, the latter having a tin ceiling with cracks in it and the occasional mouse peering through. Bernie and Miriam would raise two children, Bernard Jr. and Patricia "Patty."

Bernie's superiors took notice of the promising young Coast Guardsman, and he was often the first man called on for a mission.

Bernard C. Webber Sr. feeding a bottle to Bernard C. Webber Jr., Bayberry Cottages in Eastham, Massachusetts, in 1953. *Courtesy of Bernard C. Webber.*

In April 1950, in an early spring nor'easter, the fishing dragger *William J. Landry* was floundering near the *Pollock Rip* lightship. Guy Emro, officer in charge (OIC) of the *Pollock Rip*, spoke to the skipper of the *Landry* and alerted Alvin Newcomb. Station Chatham dispatched a lifeboat, and in the meantime the lightship crew made ready a hawser to attach to the *Landry*. Fate, however, conspired against all good intentions. The hawser idea failed. Newcomb ordered Chief Boatswain's Mate Frank Masachi to take two other men, including Bernie, to Stage Harbor, row the dory out to the mooring of the lifeboat *36383*, then hightail it to the *Landry*.

Though the *36500* at the fish pier was closer, Newcomb thought crossing the bar in a nor'easter would be too dangerous, so they opted for the longer, but safer journey in the *36383*. Twice the dory rescue crew rowed to get to the *36383*, but they capsized. The only recourse was getting back to Station Chatham, warm up and change and launch the *36500* from Old Harbor and take their chances crossing the bar. Back at the station, word came from the *Landry* that the vessel was about a half mile from the *Pollock Rip*, but it was a losing battle. The hawser was ready but the *Landry* was not close enough to grab it.

The storm worsened and the vessel went under for the last time, with all hands.

"At Chatham, in the watchroom, there was stunned silence. Four bedraggled men stood quiet, heads down, staring at the floor," Bernie remembered. "Their bodies still felt the pain and weariness of their earlier attempts to assist the *Landry*."

Chatham Bar was in constant motion, always changing. The shoals shifted making the bars awful to navigate. Breakers could "pitch-pole" a fishing vessel, which, according to Bernie, was the worst thing that could happen. "The power in the waves could pick a fishing vessel up by the stern and turn it end for end, over and over, sometimes several times, until it landed on the beach in the harbor upside down." Webber says pitch-poling meant certain death for fishermen. This is what happened to Archie Nickerson and Elroy Larkin in their forty-foot novi-boat, the *Cachalot*, on October 30, 1950, below Morris Island in Old Harbor.

Bernie, Chief Frank Masachi and Stan Dauphinais drove to the fish pier to board the *36500* and investigate. They pulled Elroy Larkin's body from the waters of Old Harbor onto the lifeboat, but the body of Arch Nickerson was never recovered. Chatham was a small world. Arch's daughter Beverly later married a seaman at Chatham, Richard Livesey, one of the four men aboard the *36500* on that February night in 1952.

That winter, Livesey helped rescue eleven crewmen from the New Bedford Scalloper *Muriel and Russell*, which ran aground at North Beach. The crew at Station Chatham used the DUKW, an amphibious relic of World War II, to rescue the crew.

Alvin Newcomb was transferred from Chatham to Woods Hole shortly after that rescue. His replacement as OIC at Station Chatham, Daniel W. Cluff, came from

Chincoteague, Virginia, and spoke with a discernible Southern accent. Cluff and Frank Masaschi butted heads and before long, Frank's request for a transfer to Woods Hole came through. Chief Boatswain's Mate Donald Bangs replaced Masaschi as OIC at Chatham and got along well with Cluff, so peace was restored there. During his years at Station Chatham, Bernie saw many men come and go.

On the morning of February 18, 1952, another nor'easter came blowing through New England. Seaman Ervin Maske from the *Stonehorse* lightship, who was born and raised in Marinette, Wisconsin, was at Station Chatham as a transient waiting for the weather to clear and hanging out in the kitchen with the cook. Richard Livesey, of Wilmington, Massachusetts, was a seaman at Chatham and Andy Fitzgerald, a Wilmington, Massachusetts native, was junior engineer.

All roads in their young lives had converged at Station Chatham for what would become a defining day in their lives with consequences, repercussions and imprints to last their entire lives.

Chapter Three

February 18, 1952
8:00 A.M.

By Theresa Mitchell Barbo

Miriam Webber was sick come dawn on February 18, 1952. "I had a real cold, flu-like" symptoms, she remembers, her vivid blue eyes alight with reflection. "I felt lousy," so she stayed at Silver Heels, the home on Sea View Avenue in Chatham she and Bernie, by now a Coast Guard bosun's mate first class (BM1), had rented in 1951.

Her husband was at Station Chatham where all hell was breaking loose. A nor'easter parted moorings, sending fishing boats on solo cruises in inlets and harbors. On orders from the OIC Daniel Cluff, Bernie recruited three guys and headed to Old Harbor to take the *36500* and tow fishing boats back to their moorings. Richard Livesey was a seaman who'd been at Station Chatham for a few months, and he helped, as did Engineman First Class Melvin F. Gouthro, the station's senior engineer.

That morning when Bernie's crew was leaving to tend to fishing boats, a call had come into the watchroom that a 503-foot oil tanker had broken in two about twenty-seven miles east of *Pollock Rip* lightship. When Bosun Cluff was ordering Bernie out to tow fishing boats, he also ordered Chief Donald Bangs to Stage Harbor where another motor lifeboat, the *36383*, would set out to assist the *Fort Mercer's* crew.

The *Fort Mercer* was a T2 SE A1, known colloquially as simply T2. The *Fort Mercer* had left Norco, Louisiana, on February 12 bound for Portland, Maine, with eight of her nine tanks loaded with kerosene and heating oil. A Coast Guard investigation would later determine that faulty construction and loading methods combined with awful weather led a "complete failure of the hull girder," and the tanker snapped in two, killing five of forty-three crewmen aboard.

It was not until Bernie, Melvin and Richard returned to Station Chatham in the middle of the afternoon that Bosun Cluff had more news for them. Unbelievably, another oil tanker with nearly identical specifications as the *Fort Mercer*, the *Pendleton*, had also broken in two and, as Bernie remembered, "and was expected to move in close somewhere along North Beach between Orleans and Chatham."

Already exhausted, already chilled to the core, Cluff gave Bernie another job: take the station's Dodge Power wagon, drive to Orleans and try to look for the *Pendleton*. "Once there we were to meet up with Roy Piggott and the Nauset Lifeboat Station crew in the amphibious vehicle DUKW. Together, we were to proceed out to Nauset Beach and attempt to locate the stricken vessel and render aid should it come ashore," Bernie explained.

Bernie's first thought was for his friend Donald Bangs, already several hours out of Stage Harbor and "how cold and miserable they must be by now."

Aboard the *Pendleton*, chaos ensued. Charles Bridges was eighteen, the youngest seaman aboard and fast asleep when the T2 tanker split in two. He awoke to grinding noises and odd vibrations and, like the rest of his shipmates, was clueless that the *Pendleton* lay in two pieces. "We had no idea the ship had broken into two," he would later say.

Charles grabbed his pants, his lifejacket and shoes and "went topside till morning," he remembered. "You couldn't see anything," said Charles, but he knew enough to tell the other guys "The other half of the ship is gone." He remembered icy decks and slid when he walked. "One guy was still asleep at 8 in the morning," Charles recounted. Charles was the sailor who went room-to-room, rousing and warning with, "Hey, you better get up. The ship's broken in two."

The snow, ice and wind made driving to Orleans hazardous, Bernie remembers, "The four-wheeled vehicle plowed on through." They met up with Piggott and his crew, and together the Coast Guardsmen set out for Nauset Beach. A hill near Mayo's Duck Farm afforded a view of the shoreline. "A brief clearing in weather showed a ship, rather a half of a ship, black and sinister, galloping up and down along huge waves, frothing each time it rose and settled back into the sea." This could be only one ship: the *Pendleton*.

The only way to get word back to Bosun Cluff at Station Chatham was to drive there, so Bernie, Melvin and Richard hightailed it back to the watch room in that Dodge Power wagon, with Piggott and his men following in the DUKW. The DUKW is a World War II–era amphibious truck with six-wheel-drive capability designed by General Motors to transport goods and troops over water and land, and the vehicles maneuver well on sand.

In the meantime, Chief Bangs and his crew found no living soul on the bow section of the *Pendleton*. According to Bernie, the pressure was on for Cluff, who had arrived in Chatham only several months before and busied himself with station renovations over boats and rescue procedures. The men who should have been in on decisions that day were unavailable or off-Cape. Alfred Volton could not get to Chatham because of the weather, and the regular group commander, Everett Marshall, was on leave.

"Cluff was from Virginia," Bernie explained. "A very Southern, nice man, but he was totally inexperienced and had absolutely no knowledge of Chatham." Now a decision needed to be made, and fast, but the man responsible for deciding "hardly knew what our boats looked like, or where Chatham Bar was…had never been out on the water," Bernie added.

In his Southern drawl, Cluff told Bernie to "'pick yourself a crew. Y'all got to take the *36500* over the bar and assist that thar ship, ya hear?'" as Bernie remembered the conversation.

Bernie looked around for three colleagues to start a mission he did not believe they would be alive to finish. Maske was in plain view while waiting patiently for transport back to *Stonehorse* lightship, passing the time in the mess hall.

"Lots of times I used to cook for them. Anything they wanted: baked dishes and pies, homemade bread…I had 'em spoiled when I was there," Ervin would say fifty years later in a quiet moment at the May 2002 reunion in Boston in the parlor of Mariners' House.

Ervin volunteered. He was just that kind of guy. "He didn't have to, he could have just looked at me and walked away, because he wasn't part of the regular Chatham crew," Bernie remembered. "Bosun Cluff ordered us out, and we went out."

Andy Fitzgerald, from Whitingsville, Massachusetts, joined the rescue team as engineer. "I doubt that I would have been considered for the *Pendleton* rescue, except we were short handed and for the fact that EN1 Melvin Gouthro became sick upon returning from Orleans, and because of other rescue attempts that day," Fitzgerald remembered in an e-mail exchange with Captain Webster. "One of the other enginemen was sick and the last one was on leave. Fate is funny sometimes."

Richard Livesey rounded out the crew. "We'd already been out the whole day, we knew how rough it was going to be out there, to tell you the truth, ya know, looking out at North Beach, you could see huge waves breaking on the beach," Richard remembered.

"Irving was not assigned to Chatham, so I didn't know him very well at all," Andy remembered. "I did know Richard quite well. He seemed to be a happy-go-lucky guy with a good sense of humor," Fitzgerald added. "I think our relationship was the same before and after the rescue."

Keeping warm was on the men's minds: "We had what they call 'foul weather gear,'" Richard said, "I don't remember what it was made of."

Some have said the regular station crew took cover when Webber on orders from Cluff, began to field his rescue team. To this day, that rumor remains a sore topic among Coast Guardsmen. Bernie says little about that, but fifty years later, Webber recalled his reaction to Cluff's order over a bacon and eggs breakfast with Andy. "Well, let's put it this way, Andy, there was a lot of guys left on that station that hadn't even been out all day long. You were still in view and available; where was everybody else?"

Within minutes Bernie, Andy, Ervin and Richard headed to Old Harbor to board the *36500* for a second time that day. They were already freezing. That an untested leader ordered them out over the notorious bar to almost certain death was not lost on the crew.

"We'd been out the whole time, the whole day, we knew how rough it was going to be out there, to tell you the truth, ya know, from looking at the shore out, you could see the waves breaking on the beach," Richard remembered.

"It was logical for me to be the one to make this attempt. After all I knew the waters and the territory better than anyone else at the station," said Bernie. Webber thought of Miriam, home sick in bed. At the fish pier, while preparing to board the dory to row out to the moored rescue boat, Bernie bumped into a neighbor, fisherman John Stello. "Call Miriam and let her know what's going on," Bernie asked him.

"You guys better get lost before you get too far out," Stello called out.

It was 5:55 p.m.

Chapter Four

FEBRUARY 18, 1952
6:00 P.M.

BY THERESA MITCHELL BARBO

As we sailed down the harbor it was dark," Bernie remembered fifty years later. By then, Bernie, Andy, Ervin and Richard were "freezing cold and soaking wet," and the mission was only in its infancy.

Webber could not believe that Daniel Cluff ordered the *36500* over the bar and into the lap of a nor'easter. As they neared the bar the crew radioed the watch room several times to confirm orders. "This is where they're gonna tell us to turn around," says Webber, but instead Bosun Cluff said, "Proceed as directed, those are your orders."

What Bernie did not know was the iron faith Andy Fitzgerald had in his coxswain. "I don't think anyone at the station could get over the bar better than Bernie."

"I've been in and out over that bar hundreds of times and never in anything like this," explained Webber in 2002. "There are people who can discuss these things and argue them six ways to Sunday," he added. "Most of them who put up the greatest questions are those who never went to sea. It's hard to imagine certain things and this is one of them."

The memories at the beginning of the journey for Bernie were that he would not survive, and those details are with him still. "The first sea over the bar hit us, picked us up, turned us around and threw us back into the harbor," Bernie recounted, as cleanly as if the memory was as fresh as rain. "Breaking seas over the lifeboat in through the windshield opening along with the violent motion of the boat tore the compass from its mount," remembered Bernie. To add to their worries, "the windshield was smashed in shattering into a million pieces," Bernie added.

Still, they motored into the black, biting night.

"When we first headed out of the harbor, Bernie asked me to man the search light in the forward compartment," Andy explained. "When we hit the first big waves starting over the bar I was lifted off my feet, as the others probably were, too. I don't remember

The bow of the hulk of the SS *Pendleton*. *Courtesy of the U.S. Coast Guard and Bernard C. Webber.*

anyone being swept out of the boat, but we were all very busy trying to keep on our feet and it could have happened without me seeing it." Fortunately, all the *36500* crewmembers remained on the vessel.

There was "so much foam," Livesey would say fifty years later. "The Lord above was looking down on us, and finally got out there after water broke on us and the windshield busted." The seas were "really big," he added, and the crew had doubts they were going to "make it."

"I don't know how the other three hung on, I really don't, because I was strapped in," Bernie remembered, using his hands to motion how the strap held him to the wheel. It would "go around your waist and hook in on the other side so I'm like this, you know," he said, virtually reenacting the posture. "Four guys back aft in that little cockpit all trying to stand in that coxswain flat and hang on to the rail there, I mean that's crowded, I don't know how they did it, because the way we were being thrown around," said Webber.

Had the seas claimed Richard, Andy or Ervin, who were wearing life jackets, Bernie thinks, "They would have at least found them dead, frozen, but floating." Bernie was unable to wear a life jacket. "It would have been too confining," he remembers.

"After we got over the bar the boat rocked and rolled, but it wasn't violent enough to lift us off the deck, and I thought we'd be okay if it didn't get worse," clarified Andy.

It did get worse. The seas became a battlefield, and the waves were relentless in their attack on the *36500*. No one said much as the hunt for the *Pendleton* began, except for Ervin, who sang hymns. Perhaps bone-deep fear rendered the *36500* crew mute and Bernie said the men did not complain much. "I'd tell them to 'watch out for this,' or, 'hang on.' Sometimes you'd go up on a sea, and I knew by the time we'd get to the top of it, we were gonna go somewhere when we'd get to the other side of it," Bernie recalled. "Then the next sea would hit you and pick you up in the air."

Some parts of Chatham Harbor and Nantucket Sound are shallow, and Bernie said when "you hit bottom, you come down off a sea and boom to the bottom and there you'd stop."

To be sure, the seas were angry, and talk of sixty-foot-high waves has become part of the tapestry of the *Pendleton* story.

Fifty years later, Bernie would say, "I've never made any claim about anything. There were enough other people talking, in fact. Nobody ever asked me," he clarified.

"Listen, the only way I know," Webber added, "I mean, I know how bad it was, where they get this forty feet, sixty feet, are from ships that were offshore. They have instruments that measure these things. And there were many different ships out there from different agencies. A navy vessel out there, three or four Coast Guard vessels out there, a couple of merchant ships out there, and all of them, with their sophisticated equipment were making weather and sea condition reports," Bernie explained.

"I know that sounds high," he offered, when asked about the sixty-foot-high waves, but "I've seen them in the North Atlantic one hundred feet high."

That night, though, the night of February 18, 1952, the twenty-three-year-old seaman steered the *36500* without a compass into the blackness, looking for a ship. "It seemed like forever, but actually I made very good time."

Divine intervention, dead reckoning and plain luck have all been trumpeted as ways Bernie's crew found the *Pendleton* that night. When asked, however, Bernie simply says, "Don't know. First I knew of it, I heard it, this rumbling, crashing, banging sound over the wind and the sea. And I sensed 'Geez, there's something there.'"

If the seas and wind knocked out the compass and windshield, left intact was the small searchlight, which proved a godsend.

"I had a crewman go forward and turn on the searchlight," Bernie said. "Also, one could hear a hissing sound," from the *Pendleton*, Bernie said, "almost like a screeching hissing sound. I think it was every time it went down into the sea with all the metal hanging off it, it created this noise. Very hard to explain, but I just knew something was there."

The searchlight combed ahead, "I was looking right into where it was broken in half. Just a white crawling mess and it would just rear up high in the water, then settle back down with a crashing and a banging. I don't know how otherwise I'd found it, I just heard it."

Bernie credits chance for the find.

"Luck, cuz I was trying to find *Pollock Rip* lightship…so I'd know where I was, and know I was off-shore in deep enough water, and then take it from there. Nobody knew where the *Pendleton* was." Not even Coast Guard Station Chatham.

"Chatham Radar didn't know where the *Pendleton* was. If Chatham Radar knew where the *Pendleton* was and knew where we were, they could have helped us find it. But they never helped us," Bernie continued. "I had nothing really to say, and they didn't say anything to me, I could have talked to them, but we were just making our way long, hanging on."

Bernie said,

> *I went down to the port side* [the left side] *and there were no lights on and the railings up there were kind of bent and smashed and I could see signs of damage, and I says, "Geez, maybe no one's on board, there's no lights on or anything…"*
>
> *As I found the stern, and I made out the name* Pendleton, Wilmington, Delaware, *so I knew for sure now what I'd found. Went around to the starboard side and by God there were lights on, deck lights shining a little yellow glow up there.*

"The wreck was impressive and scary looking but I never thought we would be swallowed by it," Andy remembered, adding, "I'm sure I would have been petrified if I thought that was going to happen." The fresh hulk towered over the small *36500*, said Andy. "I wondered how we would get anyone off if they were still alive."

"I saw one man, he looked about the size of an ant, standing at the rail," said Bernie. "My first reaction was 'Holy shit, we came all this way for one guy! Four of us, we came for one guy!'"

"I'm thinking to myself, 'How am I gonna get him off? He's gonna have to jump, it's high up in the air, say thirty feet. And, when the ship would rise, it would be more,'" Bernie remembered.

The stern of the stricken SS *Pendleton. Courtesy of the U.S. Coast Guard and Bernard C. Webber.*

"I did crawl up to the cockpit as we approached the *Pendleton* in case lines were going to be thrown to us," said Andy. "It was soon apparent that this would not work. We were bobbing up and down so much any lines would have immediately snapped."

Webber's crew did not have to think on that question too long. "Well, a few seconds later they started coming out from inside the cabin there, they all came out and lined the rail, they threw over a Jacob's ladder. And I looked at it and I'm thinking to myself, 'Maybe we ought to get off this lifeboat and get on that ladder and climb up, but before I could think much more about it, they started coming down, they wanted off.'"

"I saw them drop a ladder over the side and they started down. I then crawled back to the other compartment to see if I could help grab them as they jumped," explained Andy. "Richard and Irving came to the compartment to help them, too."

The rescue mission—the actual evacuation of humans from the mortally wounded T2 tanker—had begun, but the danger was far from over. Bernie described the situation:

> *I had to make several passes. Those guys at the bottom of the ladder, there had to be two or three others somewhere on that ladder. Well, you could only get one guy at a time off that ladder, and I'd have to judge and see. If I got in there at the wrong time, I could come up underneath him, with the lifeboat and hurt him badly. On the other hand, if I came in on the back of the sea, I could run right into him as the ship rolled and he went down and I come in off the sea I could hit him. So I had to be careful to try to get the life boat in there, get it near him, and wait for the right moment and put it ahead so he could jump…we'd be close enough for him to jump, and just hope that the guys grabbed him, which mostly they did.*
>
> *Sometimes I'd make three or four passes for one guy.*

The seas thundered and black waves rolled the *36500*, but a kind fate held as the *Pendleton* crew, one by one, made ready for their rescue.

"I remember the guys started jumping into the water, and as they were jumping into the water we'd get a hold of them, pull them aboard the boat," remembered Livesey. "I can remember doing that, time and time again."

"First you only saw one, then ya seen a whole bunch of 'em there, than ya start loading 'em on," Ervin remembered.

"As they came aboard we literally stuffed them into the covered forward compartment. After a while, they overflowed out of the covered portion and were all around us. When the compartment filled up they went to the stern area around Bernie and some went into the engine compartment," Andy clarified.

Bernie remained strapped to the wheel, and Andy, Richard and Ervin struggled to get the soaking cold merchantmen aboard the *36500*.

"If you hadn't been there, half of those guys wouldn't be here," Bernie would say to Andy half a century later. "I know that for a fact, because I was in a perfect position to look at what was going on, and Ervin worked like heck, but somebody had to set the pace and lead the troops, and that's the guy who did it," and having said that, Bernie pointed a finger right at Andy. "Somebody had to have the strength and know what to do and when to do it. A lot of guys would be hanging on themselves, afraid they'd be going overboard."

Steering and maneuvering the *36500* for each pass off the *Pendleton*'s stern was arduous. A coxswain "needed three hands to operate it," Bernie explained. "One hand to steer, my left hand, and with your right hand there was a lever that you pushed forward to put in gear, and pulled back to go into reverse, all the while operating the throttle."

Bernie had to keep the "throttle separate from that which controlled the speed of the engine. So you pushed the lever ahead, move the boat ahead, and rev up the engine, when backing down, throttle the engine down before pulling the level out of gear so you wouldn't strip the transmission out of the boat." Coordination was critical, and over time, Bernie's many trips on the *36500* made the driving of the vessel "second nature to him."

Each *Pendleton* crewman required at least one pass, and sometimes Bernie had to make several passes to get one man aboard. "Just to maneuver up alongside, it required constant work with your left hand steering, with your right hand throttling in and out of gear back and forth," he remembered. "I mean, it was work, it took a lot of effort."

"We couldn't even hear each other," Bernie recalled, and Ervin, Andy and Richard used hand signals to communicate with one another. "They knew when I started easing up to a man on the ladder, timing it right, they stood by prepared to pick the guy up if he landed on decks or in the water."

The merchantmen on the *Pendleton* cooperated fully and since they worked the high seas there was little panic on their part. Charles Bridges, a crewman aboard the *Pendleton*, remembers the *36500* would "come in and somebody would drop off, then the wave would take it out, and it would come in again." Bridges does not remember anyone being scared and "I guess we all had the same feeling: whatever is going to happen, is going to happen."

Though small, the *36500* was perfect for this rescue. "It had to be a small life boat, because no other large ship could get near the *Pendleton*," Bernie insisted. "All I can remember is some of them hit the forward deck, it's curved, it's a turtle back, and my crew grabbed hold of them," Bernie said, adding "those who fell into the sea were grabbed by my crew." He likened the motion to a fisherman "slinging a bunch of tuna fish aboard."

The workspace was tight and one by one, the *Pendleton* men were crammed in everywhere and anywhere on the *36500*, which carried a maximum safety rating for twelve, including the crew. "Shove 'em in the forward compartment, shoving them down in the engine room, and once that got full, filled them in behind me in the canvas strongback."

Thirty-three crewmen were aboard the *Pendleton* when the *36500* pulled up alongside the stern and the Jacob's ladder was flung over the side. Thirty-two were rescued. The memory of one man's death, however, would haunt all four *36500* crewmen fifty years later.

"We killed a guy so that took an awful lot" out of the crew, Bernie said, pausing, then uttering, "I remember everything" in a tone that suggested he wished he had forgotten everything, but never would.

"I'd seen death before, I'd seen a lot of people killed on the bar in Chatham and in other incidents and so forth, but nothing that stood out quite like that," Bernie remembered.

At over three hundred pounds, George "Tiny" Myers belied his nickname. Myers, a common seaman, lumbered down the Jacob's ladder. "He was as far as the crew and as far as the records go, the last one down," Bernie reflected.

Tiny Myers began climbing down the Jacob's ladder and Bernie caught sight of him, a married man with a young son. "What a strange sight in the middle of a Northeast storm out to sea in a ship that's broke in half, and here comes a fella, very heavy, with barely anything on." George Myers wore no life jacket. Bernie said he could not "understand to save my soul."

Myers "hit the boat and slid off into the water," and in Bernie's memory Tiny Myers was dying yet again. "I think Andy said he had a hold of him, but somehow or other, Tiny let go."

"The fella that died" has never left Andy. "I see him lots of times in the water," Fitzgerald recalled fifty years later.

"We couldn't help him and he couldn't help himself," said Bernie. Richard and Ervin rushed to help Andy with Tiny, before Myers let go. "It looked to me like he'd just fallen into the water off the ladder coming from the ship, and we reached down to grab him, all the other guys seemed like we could get 'em, pull them up quick, but Tiny we couldn't," remember Richard. "I had a hold on him but I couldn't hold on to him," Ervin said.

"I see his eyes looking right at me," Bernie recounted. "I could look at you and I could see his eyes, and actually the message I was getting was 'It's okay.' Somehow or other I get that."

"I'm looking at him there, and I'm trying to get in there to get him. The hull of that ship curved right down to where the propeller and the rudder were, and he was right down in there by that propeller," Bernie said.

Then a wave pushed the *36500* into the *Pendleton*'s hull, crushing Tiny, and Ervin's grip on Myers was gone.

"Then he got crushed and my fingers were all black and blue the next day," Ervin remembered. "They were crushed right alongside cuz I had to hold him when it happened. Yeah, when you get hit like that across the chest—all he did was, 'uh,' he hit pretty hard and he must have crushed every bone in his body. My fingers got all black and blue the next day."

"The wave picked us up, and Tiny grabbed hold of a line on the boat, but the wave picked us up and threw us," recounted Richard. "The next time I looked, he was floating away."

The Coast Guardsmen were devastated by Tiny's sudden, horrific death, but there were still twelve men aboard the *Pendleton* waiting for rescue and transfer to an already overcrowded boat.

"And that's why, from my perspective, after that happened, it was very difficult to go get the next guy, cuz the boat was already loaded, it might have been say, twenty men on there already, and very loaded, very heavy, not handling too well, and having gone through that, the next guy over there on the top, really feeling, 'Geez, do I dare go pick him off, because the same thing might happen again. And again. And again. But, we did," Bernie recounted.

"The thing is deciding how to go for broke, I mean, how are you gonna leave guys" aboard the *Pendleton*? Bernie wondered aloud fifty years later. "Thank God it wasn't fifty" men, he added.

"Fitzgerald was in the engine room and Livesey was in that one compartment forward of the steering area," remembered Ervin. "I was in the back end with Webber by the radio."

In a seemingly lucky stroke of Providence, Bernie said "after I got the last guy off, all of a sudden that ship came down at us, just like this," he said, motioning with his hand, "and it dawned on me, 'that ship is gonna capsize and take us all,' then the *Pendleton* rose up, rolled hard to port and disappeared" without capsizing the Coast Guard vessel.

"There we were, alone, in the darkness." Bernie remembered thinking. "Where are we?"

Chapter Five

February 18, 1952
Between 8:00 p.m. and 11:00 p.m.

By Theresa Mitchell Barbo

I don't know where we are," Bernie thought, as he steered the overloaded *36500* toward shore, but which way was shore? Bernie assumed they had headed northwest.

"What I did was to quarter the sea to get the easiest ride—if you go with the sea you've got these mountains rolling up behind you which can push you ahead and put you on the back of the sea and the next thing you're diving down into one you could bury the boat."

Bernie steered at an angle because "if you go broadside to the sea then you've got them all crashing on your side, so you can just kind of ride along with them, and that's what I was doing."

"The boat was awfully heavy and low in the water, we had so much weight on board, the seas were following behind, rolling right over the top of us," recounted Richard. "You'd go up to the sea, you come up and you come down fairly quickly. The water was constantly swirling around us. From where I was standing, with merchant seamen all around me, I couldn't move, they couldn't move."

However, to Andy, there was hope. "I felt at that time the worst was over and we were heading back and we were gonna be okay."

Bernie radioed Station Chatham to report in. "I had told them that I had thirty-two survivors from the tanker *Pendleton* on board and I was trying to make my way back in," he remembered. "But before they could almost answer me, two or three of the Coast Guard cutters that were further off shore—I don't know where they were—started giving me orders to bring the survivors out to them, and then there were arguments between them, and all kinds of conversations going on."

Bernie was upset that "there was the questioning who had more say, seniority among the cutters offshore as to how and what decisions were being made."

"Everyone can hear ya on the one channel you're on," said Ervin, who stood at Bernie's side when all this was going on.

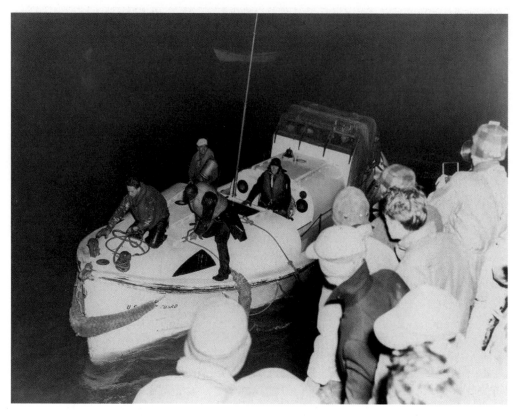

The *36500* arrives at the Chatham fish pier. *By Richard C. Kelsey.*

"They wanted me to bring the survivors out to the larger ships—'Bring them out to us.' Well, my first question is: 'Where are you?' and if you know where you are, tell me where I am because I don't know where I am." Webber added, "so the idea of bringing the survivors out to the larger Coast Guard cutter didn't make sense, especially because I had just gotten them off a ship that was bigger than most of the Coast Guard cutters, and I knew what it took to get them off, and I couldn't imagine what it would be like to try to put them on another ship out there in those conditions, so I disregarded what they had to say."

Exhausted, freezing and now irritated, Bernie remembered, "I hear all this crap going on, I shut the radio off." He remembered, "I shut off the radio so as not to be placed in the position of being directed to do what I knew was a bad decision on their part."

Later, Bosun Cluff informed Webber that disciplinary action was a possibility, along with a court-martial, because "there were some ranking officers who didn't take kindly to the fact that I turned off my radio and made my own decisions as to what our actions and fate would be," clarified Webber. "Just because we had success and landed all the survivors at Chatham safely didn't overlook the fact that I chose to ignore higher authority," he added. Cluff told Bernie not to worry about it.

A crowd gathers at the Chatham fish pier to greet the *36500* crew and *Pendleton* survivors. *By Richard C. Kelsey.*

Above: The trip from the Fish Pier to Station Chatham took less than five minutes. *By Richard C. Kelsey.*

Opposite above: Survivors of the *Pendleton* leave the *36500* for Station Chatham. *By Richard C. Kelsey.*

Opposite below: One by one, in near-shock and very cold, crew of the *Pendleton* depart for Station Chatham. *By Richard C. Kelsey*

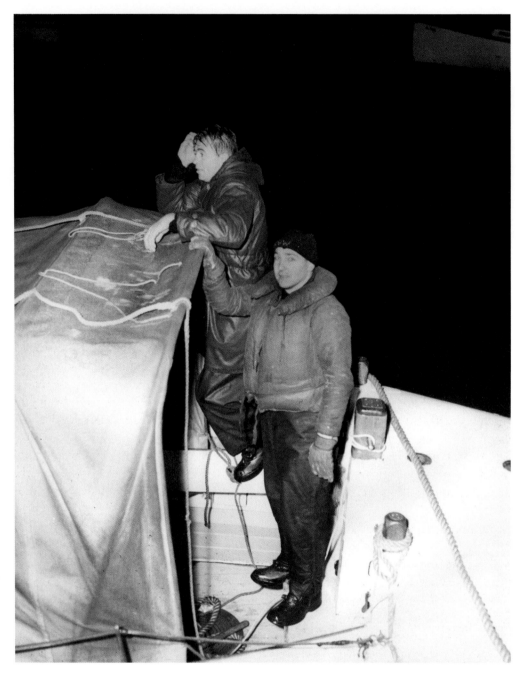

Bernie Webber and Ervin Maske on the deck of the *36500* following the harrowing rescue. *By Richard C. Kelsey.*

"I didn't know how much longer I could hang on," Bernie recalled. "I was just feeling so beat and worn, tired, wet and cold and so forth." Bernie spread the message to the *36500* crew and the *Pendleton* survivors.

> *We'll probably hit the beach somewhere, I hope it's Monomoy, but if it isn't Monomoy and I miss it altogether we're going to wind up in Nantucket Sound and Good Lord we've got all the options in the world. If we have to go all the way to Nobska Point before we hit something, my attitude was 'just find land.' I'll hold it on the beach with the engine and get off as quick as you can. Don't ask questions, get off! And hope somebody finds you.*

"We're with you, coxswain," some of the *Pendleton* crew hollered. After that, hardly anything was said.

"We were just holding on," said Richard, who was crammed in the forward compartment with the crew. "They didn't say anything," though a few prayers were muttered.

The *36500* motored into the night on the lookout for anything: lights, land or marked buoys.

Several times the humble engine sputtered out and died. "I do remember going from the front to the stern because of an engine problem," Andy recalled. "The control that had to be operated to 'prime' the engine was very close to the hot manifold and you invariably burned your arm when doing the job." Andy remembered an extremely cramped engine room. "I do believe a few of the last survivors did go into the engine compartment, because it was warmer there and not much room on the rest of the boat."

"As luck would have it, we found a little buoy on Chatham Bar" and that small red light never looked so promising before. "It was the buoy on the inside of the Chatham Bar, at the turn marking the entrance up into Old Harbor," Bernie's memoirs stated.

Bernie switched the radio back on:

> *I called the station after I got in over the bar and I told them I was rounding Morris Island and heading up the harbor and to have ambulances and help down at the pier for the survivors. I'm heading into the Fish Pier and coming down the channel between Aunt Lydia's Cove and the fish pier, and the pier was jam-packed full of people. As I looked up, I recognized many of them, many of the fishermen were there, there were little kids and women, and some of them had blankets, carrying all kinds of stuff. They helped the survivors off and scooped them up.*

"That must have been 9:00, 10:00," remembered Joe Nickerson, a carpenter and lifelong Chatham resident who high-tailed it to the fish pier that night. Earlier that day Joe heard the *Pendleton*'s distress signal as the mortally wounded tanker floated by Chatham, its stern visible from shore. "It would blow four times, then stop, four more times, then stop," remembered Nickerson.

Joe Nickerson went to Fire Chief George Goodspeed's home to report the distress call. Goodspeed in turn alerted the Coast Guard, and Nickerson says, "Bill Woodman was the radar man…and we heard conversations going back and forth."

"I never thought they'd make it, going over the bar," he remembered.

Nickerson thought seventy-five, maybe up to one hundred people crowded onto the fish pier to watch the *36500*, her crew and survivors limp into port: "They piled them right out onto the dock and right into cars," he said. "I took two of 'em down" to the Coast Guard Station in his '49 blue Ford sedan, recalled Nickerson. "They didn't say much; they were in shock."

"Long after thirty-four of the thirty-six men had left the boat, Webber stood there—exhausted, holding his head up with his elbow on the cockpit cover," photographer Dick Kelsey would say years later. "It was my most poignant photo of the night—Bernie just standing there."

Some *Pendleton* crewmen traveled to the nearby Chatham Station in Coast Guard vehicles, some of them piled into Coast Guard trucks. "I think others went in people's cars, and they drove 'em up to the station. They were right there the whole time," Bernie remembered, "like the whole town was there."

Bernie does not remember leaving the *36500* or the drive back to Station Chatham.

"We got back to the station and we had hot coffee and sandwiches and news reporters were there," remembered Richard. "Doctor Keene from Chatham had come. I think they thought we were gonna come down with pneumonia to tell ya the truth, cuz we were all soaking wet." Dr. Henry P. Hopkins, Chatham's physician of many years was there. Nickerson recalls Hopkins as a "regular guy," a World War II veteran of Guadalcanal. "He was one of the kinds of doctors who told you what was wrong with you," added Nickerson.

Radio news reporter Ed Semprini of Hyannis, eighty-nine, was at Station Chatham that evening, interviewing survivors. "I was News Director for WOCB in West Yarmouth…when we got to Station Chatham we found that all those men were not from the *Fort Mercer*, they were from the *Pendleton*," Semprini said.

Another lifelong Chatham resident, Richard Ryder, remembered that some *Pendleton* survivors weren't in the station fifteen minutes before the fainting began. They "just passed out," he remembered. "I suppose they were so relieved and keyed up," he offered. About half the *Pendleton* survivors hit the decks in a dead faint, Ryder added. "I'd never seen anything like it." All were quickly revived.

The telephone at Silver Heels rang. Miriam Webber, still sick with the flu, picked up the phone.

John Stello was on the other line. He was the fisherman who had seen Bernie at the fish pier when the *36500* headed out for the *Pendleton*.

"Did you know Bernie's a hero?" he asked.

Miriam said, "A hero, why?"

Then John Stello told Miriam about the rescue.

Chapter Six

FEBRUARY 18, 1952
11:00 P.M.
TO SPRING 1952

BY THERESA MITCHELL BARBO

After returning to Station Chatham and changing out of soaked clothing, Bernie spoke briefly to Miriam. "I can only talk a few minutes," he said, adding, "I'm fine and I'll be in touch with you tomorrow."

Hungry, Bernie headed for the galley and found a hive of activity. "As I passed through the mess hall I couldn't believe the commotion going on there," according to his memoirs. "*Pendleton* survivors were sitting, standing, and lying around the room everywhere. Some were attended to by Dr. Carroll Keene, Reverend Steve Smith, Ben Goodspeed and others, receiving medical or spiritual attention as needed."

Bernie saw the manager of Puritan Clothing in Chatham, Ben Shufro, measure *Pendleton* crewmen for new shirts and trousers. A Red Cross contingent led by Leroy Anderson helped as needed.

The rescue was big news, naturally. Ed Semprini of WOCB in West Yarmouth interviewed survivors and his interviews were aired nationally. Photographers snapped pictures of the scene. Exhausted, Bernie grabbed a bite and headed for his bunk. "All I wanted was a cup of coffee and a good Cushman's doughnut," Bernie remembered.

Once he retired, Bernie turned "thoughts and prayers were turned to those who this night remained at sea."

When Bernie woke on February 19, 1952, his life from then took a markedly different turn. "The next morning, staring at the ceiling above my bunk at the Chatham Lifeboat Station, I wondered if I had dreamed of being at sea in a storm or if I had actually taken part in the rescue of thirty-two men," Webber's memoirs stated.

Money from *Pendleton* crewmembers lay on the floor in front of Bernie's bunk, quietly placed there like an offering while he slept, a monetary expression of gratitude to the men who rescued them. Bernie gave the cash to Bosun Cluff, who bought a television for the station, quite the luxury in those days.

Radio reporter Ed Semprini interviews *Pendleton* crewmen recovering from their ordeal at Station Chatham. *By Richard C. Kelsey.*

Left to right: Bernie Webber, Andy Fitzgerald, Richard Livesey and Ervin Maske warm up with coffee and doughnuts at Station Chatham following their long night at sea. *By Richard C. Kelsey*

The *Pendleton* crewmen who survived were transported to Boston, and eventually, home. On February 19, Dick Kelsey was aboard the *36500* that went back to the bow of the *Pendleton.* "The seas were too dangerous to board," he said. "Later one body was found in the bow paint locker wrapped in burlap, rolled in sawdust and dead from exposure."

Today, Bernie is immensely respectful at the mention of so many lives being lost on the SS *Pendleton.* "Everyone on the bow died," he reminded.

> *Six days after the storm the CG 36500 was dispatched at 0945 to the bow section of* Pendleton *to remove the body of Herman G. Gatlin. The salvage crew from the tug* CURB *had found his body wrapped in rags and covered over with sawdust (normally used for oil spills) laying on a paint locker shelf where he evidently went after the ship broke in two to try to keep warm and survive. When the lifeboat arrived the salvage crew "tossed" his body over the side from high above into the boat…they refused to use the stokes-litter the Coast Guard crew brought out so that it could be lowered in a respectful manner. The handling of the one body located…was a shock to a Coast Guard crew who had a greater respect for humans alive or dead.*

That there were survivors was a reason to rejoice, but the knowledge that so many had perished within the grasp of a cold, angry sea was never lost on any Coast Guardsman at Station Chatham. "With the loss of Myers," Bernie said, "the body in the bow meant a lot, just being able to see it returned to loved ones."

In the days following the *Pendleton*'s demise, photographer Richard C. Kelsey snapped this picture of the wreck. *By Richard C. Kelsey.*

The bow of the wreck of the *Pendleton*. *By Richard C. Kelsey.*

Survivors and Casualties

The *Boston Herald* listed the names of the *Pendleton* survivors rescued by the *36500*, in order by rank, in its February 20, 1952 edition. Where available, titles and ranks were provided:

> *Ray L. Sybert, Chief Engineer, aged thirty-three, from Norfolk, Virginia; 1ˢᵗ Assistant Engineer David A. Brown; 2ⁿᵈ Assistant Engineer Edward A. Gallagher; 3ʳᵈ Assistant Engineer Douglas B. Potts; 3ʳᵈ Assistant Engineer Wallace P. Quirey; Mike Faifua, Boatswain; Frederick Onno; Charles W. Bridges; Junior J. Hicks; James E. Young, Pump Man; Edward C. Brown, engineer Room Maintenance Man; Tchuda W. Southerland, Oiler; Vernon A. Collins, Oiler; Frank Fateux, Fireman; Aaron B. Povsell, Wiper; Joseph W. Zezptarski, Mess Man; Albert L. Johnson, Oiler; Henry Anderson, Wiper; Margasito T. Flores, Galley Man; Rollo E. Kennison, Deck Maintenance Man; Raymond G. Stelle; Lorand David Maillbo, Utility Man; Oliver Gendron, Steward; Fred Baker, Fireman; Alfred S. Baltazar, Chief Clerk; Arthur Schuster, Fireman; Alfred S. Baltazar, Chief Clerk; Arthur Schuster, Fireman; Domingo F. Garcia, Messman; Gerald Lee Russell, Deck Maintenance Man; Eldon C. Hanan, Deck Maintenance Man; Aquinol B. Oliveira, 2ⁿᵈ cook; Carrol M. Kilgore, Messman; Fred R. Brown, Wiper.*

The Herald listed George Myers (Tiny) as "Lost during rescue."

In a report dated September 25, 1952, from the chief of the Merchant Vessel Inspection Division, H.C. Shepard, to the chief of the Officer of Merchant Marine Safety, the names of nine crewmembers aboard *Pendleton* who perished on February 18, 1952, were given:

> *John J. Fitzgerald, Master*
> *Martin Moe, Chief Mate*
> *Joseph W. Colgan, Second Mate*
> *Harold Bancus, Third Mate*
> *James G. Greer, Radio Operator*
> *Joseph L. Landry, A.B. Seaman*
> *Herman G. Gatlin, A.B. Seaman*
> *Billy Roy Morgan, Ordinary Seaman*
> *George D. Myers (Tiny), Ordinary Seaman*

Included in the same report is the suspected cause of the *Pendleton* disaster: "In arriving at its determinations of the cause of this casualty the Board based its opinions on three principal factors which contributed mainly to the breaking in two of the *PENDLETON*, namely: (1) construction, (2) weather and (3) loading."

The Coast Guard pointed to the "many points of stress concentration in the *PENDLETON*," which contributed to its demise. Weather was blamed, too. "The

An official Coast Guard portrait of BM1 Bernard C. Webber. *Courtesy of the U.S. Coast Guard and Bernard C. Webber.*

First Coast Guard District Admiral James Bradbury with BM1 Bernard C. Webber in May 1952. *Courtesy of the U.S. Coast Guard and Bernard C. Webber.*

BM1 Webber (far left) at a Boston Kiwanis Club Luncheon in 1952. Admiral J. Bradbury is at center. *Courtesy of the U.S. Coast Guard and Bernard C. Webber.*

Board is of the opinion that the weather had a vital part in causing this casualty particularly the temperature and the sea…and the probable position of the vessel with reference to the direction of the seas would at times place the bow and stern portions of the vessel in the crests of waves with little or no support amidships." As for loading, the Coast Guard's report concluded an imbalanced cargo—with some tanks empty and others full—caused a weight shift that contributed to the accident.

The report also stated, "The loss of George Myers during the evacuation of the stern section was not due to any lack of effort on the part of the Coast Guard, or to defective equipment on the tanker."

After the *Pendleton* rescue, Webber evolved into the Coast Guard's "hero poster boy." In the 1950s, as America slid past the postwar years, the mentality and culture of the Armed Forces was to tout its heroes. Bernie made numerous appearances on behalf of the Coast Guard following the *Pendleton* rescue. There were "many talks to the Kiwanis and Rotary Clubs around Cape Cod and Boston, and the Propeller Club in Boston," remembered Bernie.

Above: BM1 Bernard Webber awaits a public relations assignment at the Touraine Hotel, Boston, in 1952. *Courtesy of the U.S. Coast Guard and Bernard C. Webber.*

Right: U.S. Coast Guard Commandant Merlin O'Neil and BM1 Bernard C. Webber at the Great Southern Hotel in Baltimore, Maryland, where Webber was the recipient of the American Legion Medal of Valor and Coast Guardsman of the Year, 1952. *Courtesy of the U.S. Coast Guard and Bernard C. Webber.*

BM1 Webber at the American Legion Dinner in Baltimore in 1952. *Courtesy of the U.S. Coast Guard and Bernard C. Webber.*

Miriam Webber (far left) was also invited to the American Legion Dinner in Baltimore in 1952. *Courtesy of the U.S. Coast Guard and Bernard C. Webber.*

BM1 Webber addresses the audience at the Baltimore event. *Courtesy of the U.S. Coast Guard and Bernard C. Webber.*

The commandant of the U.S. Coast Guard, Merlin O'Neil, at the Great Southern Hotel in Baltimore, with BM1 Webber, 1952. *Courtesy of the U.S. Coast Guard and Bernard C. Webber.*

Edward R. Mitton (left), president of the Jordan Marsh Co., presents Jordan's "Award of Merit" medals to heroic Coast Guardsmen for outstanding bravery in the *Pendleton* disaster. Mitton gives medals to (left to right) Captain W.R. Richards, chief of staff, First Coast Guard District, who accepted for eight of ten men unable to attend; Bernard C. Webber, BM1; and Daniel W. Cluff of Station Chatham. *Courtesy of Bernard C. Webber.*

Bernard C. Webber, twenty-three, BM1, is congratulated by Under Secretary of the Treasury Edward H. Foley after being presented with the Treasury Department's Gold Lifesaving Medal in Washington, D.C., for his "extreme and heroic daring" in the recent *Pendleton* rescue. *Courtesy of the U.S. Coast Guard and Bernard C. Webber.*

Webber stayed at the Touraine Hotel in Boston to take part in Armed Forces Day activities. He traveled to Baltimore, Maryland, and stayed at the Great Southern Hotel for the American Legion Medal of Valor Banquet where he was honored as the Coast Guard Man of the Year in 1952. There were many photo ops with "Senators, Commandant of the USCG, other Admirals and Generals," noted Bernie.

On April 15, 1952, Bernie received an invitation from Edward R. Mitton, president of the Jordan Marsh Company, to "be one of our Head Table guests at the Jordan Marsh luncheon" held on April 28, "in honor of Cape Cod and the Islands, and including a salute to Coast Guard personnel on the Cape." Mitton presented Bernie with the Award of Merit at the event held at the Parker House in Boston.

On May 14, 1952, twenty-one Coast Guardsmen, including Bernie, Andy, Ervin and Richard, were honored for heroism for the rescue of seventy men from the *Fort Mercer* and *Pendleton* tankers. The Coast Guard's Congressional Gold Lifesaving Medal, which is the Coast Guard equivalent to the Congressional Medal of Honor, was given to each *36500* crewmember by the Under Secretary of the Treasury Edward H.Foley.

Under Secretary of the Treasury Edward H. Foley, *left*, congratulates Seaman Ervin Maske, of Marinette, Wisconsin, after presenting him with the Gold Lifesaving Medal at a ceremony held in Washington, D.C., on May 15, 1952. Behind Maske (left to right) are (first row) Engineman Second Class Andy Fitzgerald, Ensign William R. Kiely Jr., Seaman Richard Livesey and BM1 Bernard C. Webber (second row) Chief Bosun Mate Donald H. Bangs, Seaman Richard J. Ciccone, Engineman First Class Emory H. Haynes and Engineman First Class John F. Dunn. *Courtesy of the U.S. Coast Guard and Bernard C. Webber.*

At the decoration ceremony on May 14, 1952, Vice Admiral Merlin O'Neill delivered these remarks:

> *February 18 and 19 always will be remembered in Coast Guard history. On those two days a nor'easter swept New England. It was bitter cold…with snow and sleet and howling winds. East of Cape Cod 70-knot winds and 60-foot seas battered merchant vessels which had not been able to make port. This was the setting for the Coast Guard drama which we review here today. Two larger tankers appeared on the scene—the SS* Fort Mercer *and the SS* Pendleton. *Forty miles apart, they met the full and awful force of the storm. They broke in two on the morning of February 18…and the four separate hulks were swept along at the mercy of the sea. Survivors were marooned on each hulk…a total of 84 half-frozen men whose chances for rescue seemed impossible. The story of how 70 of these men were snatched from the elements and delivered safely ashore made headline news for several days. We have gathered here today to honor some of the men who took part in the* FORT MERCER–PENDLETON *rescue operations.*

Massachusetts Senator Leverett speaks to *36500* crewmen Andy Fitzgerald, Richard Livesey and Bernard C. Webber in Washington, D.C., on May 15, 1952. *Courtesy of the U.S. Coast Guard and Bernard C. Webber.*

I say some of these men because their individual exploits were outstanding. But we should not forget the much larger number of their shipmates whose skills, courage and devotion to duty went unnoticed in the overall operation. I am proud to say that it was the teamwork of all Coast Guard units involved that made possible the exceptional exploits that we note here today. As to individual exploits, you will hear the citations read shortly. In reality, these 21 men faced four separate rescue operations. Each operation offered special problems. But each held the same danger from hulks that tossed like corks in the towering waves. These men went about their duties drenched by icy water, without food for hours at a time…and with death riding on every wave. The operations were unique in Coast Guard history, and called for the skillful use of all types of rescue equipment…of cutters and small life-boats, of an airplane, a sea-going tug; of rubber life rafts, radar, scramble nets and exposure suits. But most of all, the situation called for raw courage and skill of the highest order—backed by true Coast Guard teamwork! To you men here, and to your shipmates, let me say that the entire Coast Guard is very, very proud of you.

Only twenty-four and still new to the Coast Guard, Bernie itched to get back to Station Chatham to work, despite the honors being bestowed upon him. "I asked for a transfer out of Chatham shortly after Pendleton," he remembered, to follow Chief Frank Masaschi, who did not get on with Bosun Cluff. Frank, however, "didn't know what he was getting," said Bernie. "I was second in charge of the CG Patrol Boat *83388*...as the Coast Guard was sending me everywhere on PR missions Frank had to do extra duty on board the boat as I wasn't available to relieve him," he recounted. "It didn't sit well with him or the crew for me to be gone so much."

Bernie continued his Coast Guard duties through the rest of the 1950s and '60s, including a tour in Vietnam. "The Coast Guard cutter *Point Banks*, skippered by Boston-born Chief Petty Officer Bernard C. Webber, 37, is among 17 patrol boats being assigned by the United States to sea duty off South Viet Nam," reported the *Boston Globe* on Friday, April 30, 1965. The Department of Defense had planned on sending two hundred specially trained Coast Guardsmen to man the eighty-two-foot cutters, primarily used for search and rescue missions, which were capable of extended sea duty, yet drew only about five feet of water.

Bernie's family was upset by the military orders. "Mrs. Webber...said her husband was planning to retire next March after 20 years service," the *Globe* reported. "Reverend Alonzo Webber...the Coast Guardsmen's father, said today that his son had already made plans with two other men to operate a marina in Chatham. He said his son had just returned from a two-week trip at sea," the paper added. After Vietnam, Bernie would retire in 1966.

Fifty years to the month of the May 1952 Gold Medal Decoration Ceremony, the Coast Guard would again honor Bernie Webber, Andrew Fitzgerald, Richard Livesey and Ervin Maske.

Chapter Seven

TUESDAY, MAY 14, 2002

BY THERESA MITCHELL BARBO

Vibrant sapphire skies and intermittent clouds on May 14, 2002, over the Lower Cape, belied an Arctic-like cold. However, Station Chatham laid out the warmest of welcomes for its former crew when Bernie, Andy, Ervin and Richard, along with Charles Bridges, came to call.

Around nine o'clock, following breakfast at Chatham Wayside Inn and the dinner held there the night before, the Gold Medal Crew met at the Chatham fish pier for a memorial ride in the restored *36500*, where fifty years before, in a February nor'easter, they had carried the *Pendleton* rescued to safety. Junior Coastguardsmen measured and buckled Bernie, Andy, Ervin and Richard into regulation orange jackets. Charles Bridges was not aboard. Off they went, albeit, awkwardly. Bernie recounted,

> *To be perfectly honest, I hadn't had a chance to talk with Ervin, Andy, Richard or Charlie. People who plan these events don't realize it's a swirl of activities and those in the spotlight are overwhelmed by events. Little thought goes into realizing these guys haven't been together or seen each other for more than fifty years. It was an awkward situation. Inasmuch we were not a boat crew, but were guests aboard 36500 for a photo op.*

Despite the initial awkwardness, as he had done on February 18, 1952, Bernie took the tiller, and that "seemed perfectly normal," he remembered.

Master Chief Jack Downey, along with Senior Chief Sheila Lucey, officer-in-charge of Brandt Point Station on Nantucket, tagged along in case the *36500* crew needed a helping hand. "I got the impression those in charge had preplanned that I not be allowed to bring the boat into the fish pier," Bernie said in January 2007. "I assume the thinking was that the old man was rusty and it best to be on the safe side to let another take over," but he did well that day.

The *36500* Gold Medal crew outside Station Chatham in May 2002. *Courtesy of Bernard C. Webber.*

Andy Fitzgerald, Senior Chief Steve Lutjen, Ervin Maske, Richard Livesey and Bernie Webber at Chatham's Fish Pier, May 2002. *Courtesy of Theresa Mitchell Barbo.*

Lucey does not remember much conversation, but the poignancy of the moment was not lost on anyone underway on the *36500*. "It was awesome to see and watch him handle the boat that he saved so many lives with," remembered Lucey, who called Bernie's presence a privilege.

A luncheon at Station Chatham followed in the very room where Bernie scrounged for a doughnut and coffee some fifty years before. The Gold Medal Crew gathered around a classic sheet cake and posed for pictures.

After lunch, the official Cape ceremony began with the National Anthem sung by a local North Chatham favorite, Carole Maloof. As the youngest of the four Gold Medal honorees, Andy Fitzgerald was given the duty of unveiling a bronze plaque in honor of the *36500* crew. Among the local dignitaries present were Selectman Douglas Ann Bohman and Parker Wiseman.

The First Coast Guard District chaplain, Lieutenant Commander T.A. Yuille, U.S. Navy, delivered the invocation. Giving remarks were Captain James Murray, commander of Coast Guard Group Woods Hole, and Captain Webster, who recognized that Station Chatham remains an indelible element to the town. "We also celebrate a uniquely positive relationship between the Coast Guard and the town of Chatham and other surrounding communities; a town and communities that have embraced their rich maritime past and their Coast Guard," said Webster.

The Gold Medal crew board the restored *36500* at Chatham's Fish Pier for a press photo op. In the foreground is Master Chief Jack Downey. *Courtesy of Theresa Mitchell Barbo.*

At Station Chatham in May 2002 (left to right), Bernie Webber, Andy Fitzgerald, Richard Livesey and Ervin Maske share coffee and conversation. *Courtesy of Theresa Mitchell Barbo.*

Station Chatham welcomed back its *36500* crew in May 2002: (left to right) Andy Fitzgerald, Richard Livesey, Charles Bridges, Bernie Webber and Ervin Maske. *Courtesy of Theresa Mitchell Barbo.*

It is to Captain Webster's persistence and devotion that Cape Cod Coast Guard maritime history is commemorated within the service's ranks. "I am pleased to report to the Town of Chatham, Station Chatham and Group Woods Hole that your combined efforts to highlight our…heritage have led the way in the Coast Guard and will result in an experimental pilot program that will, for the first time in fifty-seven years, see personnel assigned to the District in Boston to begin field collection and analysis of Coast Guard historical events," Webster explained.

After the speeches, when the sheet cake was polished off, the dishes cleared and most civilian guests gone, perhaps the most special event for Bernie took place. This was a slot in the schedule that did not appear on the official program.

It was Bernie's wish to speak directly to the enlisted men and women at Station Chatham without officers present. That included Captains Webster and Murray, who left the dining hall. What was said behind closed doors is not talked about today. It was an opportunity for the enlisted men to ask Bernie questions about the rescue, and the Coast Guard in general, without their superiors present. In doing so, several generational gaps were closed, for Bernie was old enough to be grandfather and even great-grandfather to some of the young men and women nearby.

During Bernie's private time with enlisted folks the captains killed time in the station. Miriam Webber and Captain Murray would speak at length in Senior Chief Lutjen's

On February 18, 1952, four crewmen from
Coast Guard Station Chatham,
in the motor lifeboat 36 500,
rescued 32 men from the wreck of the tanker
Pendleton in 60 foot seas and the dark of night.

This spectacular achievement, which is
considered the Coast Guard's greatest
peacetime rescue, was accomplished by:

BM 1	Bernard C. Webber
EN 2	Andrew J. Fitzgerald
SN	Richard P. Livesey
SN	Irving W. Maske

The Town of Chatham is proud to honor these men

May 15, 2002

A plaque honoring the *36500* crew is unveiled at Station Chatham in May 2002. *Courtesy of Theresa Mitchell Barbo.*

office with no one for company except Zoe, the station's chocolate labrador retriever mascot.

In the late afternoon, Captain Webster, Captain Murray, the Gold Medal Crew and Charles Bridges drove to the headquarters of the Orleans Historical Society for a ceremony to recognize the organization's work in restoring the *36500*. They also viewed an exhibit depicting Coast Guard history assembled by Donna and Bob Weber, a retired Coast Guard officer who served at Station Chatham and both were instrumental, along with Bonnie and Stanley Snow of Orleans, in organizing the Chatham leg of the 2002 reunion.

Soon after, the reunion officially ended. Folks picked up their official lives and scattered. Captain Murray returned to Woods Hole and Captain Webster left Cape Cod for Boston to resume duties as chief of operations for Coast Guard District One. The Gold Medal Crew returned to Chatham Wayside Inn with their families to pack for home.

A white Coast Guard Dodge van prepared to bring the *36500* Gold Medal Crew to Boston to catch flights back home, or to stay on in Boston an extra night: Andy Fitzgerald and his wife, Gloria, to Colorado; the Liveseys to Florida; Ervin Maske, with his daughter, Anita, and son, Matt, to Wisconsin; and Charles Bridges and his wife, Suellen, and daughter and sister-in-law, to Florida. Bernie and Miriam would stay on

Captain W. Russell Webster addresses the *36500* crew and guests at Station Chatham in May 2002. *Courtesy of Theresa Mitchell Barbo.*

Bernie Webber leaves Station Chatham at the end of the reunion in May 2002. *Courtesy of Theresa Mitchell Barbo.*

Bernie Webber's family relaxes with his family in at Squire Restaurant in Chatham after the reunion: (left to right) son-in-law Air Force Major Bruce Hamilton, granddaughter Hilary Hamilton, Bernie, granddaughter Leah Hamilton, Miriam Webber and daughter Patricia "Patty" Webber Hamilton.

at Miriam's sister's home in Eastham, which Bernie helped build decades ago. Bernie needed to relax and rest.

Ervin's daughter, Anita Maske Jevne, said her father loved seeing everyone again after fifty years. Anita never heard Ervin talk of the February 18, 1952 rescue. Once, when she was little, Ervin showed her his medal and explained that "I got this medal from a rescue I did…I saved some men." Until the Heroes Luncheon in Boston that Monday, Anita had never heard the full story.

I found Ervin sitting alone in the back of the Coast Guard van that afternoon waiting on his son, Matt, and daughter, Anita, to gather their things for the ride to Boston. His knees were bothering him after several long days, most of which were spent standing or walking, but the pain had subsided and he appeared to be okay, just tuckered out.

He seemed, however, full of thought, and a quiet I came to know as a reflection of a gentle soul. We talked a few minutes and Ervin said something that broke my heart: "Ya know, the guys in the garage where I worked in Wisconsin didn't believe me when I said I was on this Coast Guard mission. Now maybe they will believe me."

It occurred to me then that the May 2002 reunion, orchestrated by Captain Webster, was obviously more than a gathering of Coast Guardsmen. It was a validation of sorts for Ervin. My throat caught, and on impulse, I hugged Ervin and kissed his cheek. He said he "don't get too many of those kisses no more," and he hugged me back. I felt it was a privilege to have met him, not because of his status as a Coast Guard hero, but because he was a man of deep humility and had endured so much in his lifetime.

It was the last time I would see Ervin. Ervin Maske died on October 7, 2003, near his hometown of Marinette, Wisconsin, after suffering an apparent heart attack while at the wheel of an empty school bus. He was the first of the *36500* Gold Medal Crew to pass on. To date, Bernie, Richard and Andy are still living, as is Charles Bridges.

Anita believes it was Captain Webster who had arranged for the Coast Guard Honor Guard to attend Ervin Maske's funeral. "The Honor Guard came, and there was a gun salute," Anita remembered speaking by phone from her home in Eau Claire, Wisconsin. "They gave me the flag and inside were three shells from the gun salute." Anita kept one and gave two to her brother, Matt, who came for the reunion and shared that special time with their father.

"The man who handed me the flag…he was crying," Anita recounted, and I could hear own her tears through the phone line.

"The reason why we are here is because we are taking your Dad's honor with us, so it will always be alive," a young Coast Guardsman explained to Anita.

Chapter Eight

January 2007
A Wide Circle Closes

By Theresa Mitchell Barbo

After fifty-five years the story of Bernie Webber and the *36500* rescue of the *Pendleton* crew might be boiled down to a few sentences: "It was a case of survival," Bernie said, "not only for the survivors of the *Pendleton* but for us. There were no heroics," he added.

Nothing but the need to see daylight the next morning sustained the crew that night. "We all wanted to survive. I actually never thought we would," Bernie recalled. "The job is like a soldier. You go into battle; you don't think it's going to be a dance."

Until a few years ago, however, the gaping wounds that christened Bernie as a hero, albeit a reluctant one, in 1952, appeared not to have healed entirely. "This business of being called a hero is really a life wrecker," he lamented in recent years.

Hard feelings on behalf of his peers simmered after the February 1952 rescue, and to a degree this still rankles Bernie. "After the *Pendleton* I still had the rest of my Coast Guard career to finish," recounted Webber. People thought Bernie benefited from the publicity, an accusation that stung for decades. "When they see something that was written…money went into my pocket," he said many had assumed. "Most of the guys I had in charge of me resented me…a very difficult career," Webber remembered.

"I felt much animosity after '52 for the remainder of my career until retirement in 1966, coming from both enlisted and officers," he said.

Since 1952, Bernie thinks newer generations who served in the 1970s and 1980s seem "to have a growing dislike for 'cussed-Yankee types' like myself. All the hoopla hasn't helped," Webber explained, adding, "However, I find among the younger generation I seem to be accepted and feel most comfortable."

Each decade since 1952 seemed to have torn a fresh wound into Webber. Haunting Bernie is a conversation he heard only a few years ago when retired Chief Bosun Mate Ralph O. Morris, seventy-two, who worked for Bernie while Webber ran the Race Point Station in Provincetown in 1955, visited Bernie and Miriam in Florida.

Morris told Webber of a chance encounter in Hyannis in 1953 with the widow and young son of Tiny Myers, the ordinary seaman aboard the *Pendleton* who perished during the rescue effort. The three met up in front of Puritan Clothing store when Morris dashed in to buy some civilian clothing. Coming out of the store, the Myers lad stared at the Coast Guard uniform Morris wore. Morris said the child looked to be between eight and twelve.

"Are you in the Coast Guard?"

"Yes, I'm in the Coast Guard," Morris replied.

"Do you know Bernie Webber?"

"I don't know him, but I know of him," Morris told the boy. Morris, just a year or so out of boot camp, had heard about Bernie's story during his training but had failed to connect the dots about which the Myers child was talking. Morris and Webber would not meet until several years later.

"He says to me, 'He killed my father.'"

"I didn't know at the moment, he caught me by complete surprise and shock because I had no idea who he was, where he came from, and I didn't know what story he was talking about," Morris said from his home in Texas.

Morris asked the boy how Bernie had killed his father. Mrs. Myers then stepped in and replied for her son. "His father got caught between the ship and the lifeboat when he was rescuing the people off the *Pendleton*."

Morris said he leaned over the fatherless boy and "I told the kid, 'Let me tell you something: you gotta remember there were two ships that broke up that night, and the *Pendleton* was one of them. When you're trying to rescue people in weather that would break up two ships it is almost impossible to blame anybody for losing anyone.'"

Morris called the loss of Tiny "an act of God for not the fault of any one person." Morris remains adamant that "it's a miracle they even got out of Chatham" that night.

The belief that Tiny Myers's son would have thought Bernie was guilty of taking his father's life wears on Webber today like a thick chain around his heart.

The loss of Tiny Myers affected every crewman aboard the *36500*—Livesey, Fitzgerald and the late Maske. In private moments at the *Pendleton* reunion in Boston in May 2002, each spoke of Tiny as if the loss was a fresh wound, rather than George Myers having died over fifty years ago. Even after fifty years, the crew of the *36500* remembered still the one they could not save, although they carried thirty-two others to safety. They have seen Tiny's face in their minds through the years as he reached through the freezing seas for their hands. Seeing a good man die under tragic circumstances never leaves a would-be rescuer's memory.

A second portion to the Myers story, buried under the waves of 1952, is something about which Bernie has never spoken publicly before and never will again. Tiny Myers was not the last man to scamper down the Jacob's ladder from the *Pendleton* that night, unlike what everyone was led to believe for decades.

"SS *Pendleton* Chief Engineer Raymond L. Sybert and the *Pendleton* survivors concocted the story to place Myers in the best light for his family's sake," Bernie remembered.

"For me, the fact was that after Fitzgerald let go of Myers and he was crushed by the lifeboat, I had a decision to make," he said. Bernie wrestles even today with a question: "Continue spending time trying to get Myers's body or leave him and go pick up the remaining crewmen from the ship?"

BM1 Webber left Myers to save the living. "My decision has haunted me all these years whether I did the right thing. Also, many could not understand how I lost Myers if he was the last man off, especially when I got all the others."

Bernie, nor any of the other *36500* crew, was not involved in this deceptive plan, and for fifty-five years the guys said nothing. "Bosun Cluff advised I not think about it. What was done was done," Bernie recounted. "It all just happened and I wasn't consulted."

"The truth is that Sybert himself as the ranking officer was the last man off," Bernie recounted, not George Myers.

Then, in earlier decades, there was the matter of the *36500* itself. When Bernie was notified of efforts to restore the vessel in 1973, he was enlisted to help raise funds to refurbish the *36500*, which had sat orphaned in a boatyard, rapidly decaying. "In many ways it was embarrassing, but on the other hand, I was being pressured to help them, otherwise I'd be an ingrate," said Webber.

That was then.

'Tis a new era. Today, a completely fresh crew on Cape Cod is in charge of the *36500*. Management and maintenance of the *36500* remains in the hands of the Orleans Historical Society under the auspices of Peter Kennedy who says the vessel is "in better physical condition than it's ever been." Through a new website—www.cg36500. org—Kennedy says, "We now get notes and calls from across the country…Many are from retired CG people who served on 36' motor life boats." Men and women from all branches of the military, mostly retired, though, are hands-on volunteers keenly dedicated to the *36500*.

Kennedy and Webber share a devotion to the *36500*. If the management structure of the former motor lifeboat has matured in Bernie's eyes, so has the Coast Guard over the past fifty-five years.

"One thing that should hold true to the traditions of the USCG to this day is that one should see his or her duty and do it without question," Webber insists. "I think the tradition stands as exemplified by the Coast Guard during Hurricane Katrina."

If the first five decades following the 1952 *Pendleton* rescue were an exercise in frustration, personality conflicts and anxiety for Bernie, the past five years might have made up for some of the past sorrow. It took some doing but Bernie was finally convinced to come to Boston in May 2002 for a fiftieth anniversary reunion of the *36500* crew, and to visit Station Chatham. Captain Webster promised Bernie the trip would be worthwhile and meaningful, and Bernie credits Captain Webster, who meticulously planned the reunion, for building the bridge between the Old Coast Guard and the New Coast Guard, and Bernie safely crossed over, leaving troubled waters behind.

They remain good friends today. "Webber is fully engaged in other Coast Guard–related history projects," says Captain Webster, and Bernie remains a cherished, living legend to past and current Guardsmen.

These days, from his retirement home in Melbourne, Florida, Bernie and Miriam live a quiet life, as is their wish. However, in recent years Bernie has involved himself in Coast Guard projects that relate to preserving the heritage of the service. He was, for instance, enormously helpful in assisting the artist Tony Falcone of Prospect, Connecticut, with background information over the course of two years for the beautiful mural depicting the rescue that hangs at the Coast Guard Academy in New London, Connecticut.

Falcone was commissioned to paint a series of paintings about the history of the United States Coast Guard, and was assigned a "Champion" to "get it right" since the Coast Guard was a new world to him. Bernie was Tony's Champion for the painting, entitled *36500 Rescues the MV Pendleton, 1952*.

"Not only did he know every detail of the events surrounding this incredible rescue mission, but he was the person on the scene…to say that he brought this historic event to life is an understatement," Falcone remembered.

"Working together meant that we discussed all aspects of Bernie's heroic struggle to make it to the tanker, rescuing the crewmen from both the tanker and his own vessel, one after another, and making it safely to shore." Bernie and Tony exchanged sketches and Tony recounted they went over each one, including every angle and aspect, and "how Bernie endured my endless questions, I will never know."

Falcone commented that their collaboration enabled Bernie to revisit the rescue. "After working with him, I am able to understand how a man of his character could accomplish what he did. He is truly a unique man."

In recent years, Bernie would take several trips to Nantucket to visit his friend, Senior Chief Sheila Lucey, at the Station Brandt Point. Lucey was one of two current Coasties to be on the 36500 with Webber and the Gold Medal Crew at the May 2002 Reunion in Chatham.

When he visited Nantucket, "He came out and ran the forty-seven-foot, and that was way cool watching him handle the new platform," Lucey remembered. Bernie watched their drills and performed a few of his own, to rave reviews of Lucey's crew. "He made it all about them…talked about how impressed he was with their skill…the crew couldn't have been higher."

Bernie handed the boat crew and coxswain certificates for some newly qualified members. "They couldn't believe it," Lucey recounted. "They were humbled by his presence…he has an ability to make these guys feels like they are the heroes, and what an awesome gift that is to give to a young guy just starting out."

Fifty-five years after the mortally wounded *Pendleton* wrecked, and Bernie became a hero in many eyes except his own, the circle has finally closed.

"From my observation having made trips in the last couple of years aboard Coast Guard vessels and visiting shore-stations, any beefs I had about the old days have been resolved," Webber says. "From my perspective it's a great time to be in the service, and I've never been prouder to say I had served in the United States Coast Guard."

It may have taken fifty-five years, but the circle on the *Pendleton* rescue has closed, and with peace at last, for Bernard C. Webber.

PART TWO

Chapter Nine

FOUND HEROES
GOING FOR GOLD: THE USCG'S LIFESAVING MEDALS

BY CAPTAIN W. RUSSELL WEBSTER, USCG (RET.)
ORIGINALLY PUBLISHED IN WRECK & RESCUE JOURNAL,
VOLUME 3, NUMBER 3

The Coast Guard recognizes America's heroes for their daring, and often death-defying water rescues with the prestigious Gold and Silver Lifesaving Medals. On average, five or six Gold Lifesaving Medals are given out each year to recognize extraordinary acts of heroism. About fifteen Silver Lifesaving Medals are given out annually for slightly lesser acts of courage.

These medals are like Olympic medals in one sense because they have great meaning to the recipients and those that have been saved. In another way, they are unlike Olympic medals because they recognize a single defining moment in the lives of the participants—a moment that no amount of training could prepare the participants. Some have likened the Lifesaving Medals to the prestigious Medal of Honor in terms of their rarity and importance.

They are a tribute to selfless heroism in the face of death. The process of investigating these acts, especially those acts that have gone unrecognized for many years, costs time for local Coast Guard commands, but offers unique rewards when the investigation is finally completed.

The Gold and Silver Lifesaving Medals were established in 1874 by an act of Congress, which authorized the Secretary of the Treasury to bestow the medals upon individuals who endanger their own lives in saving or endeavoring to save lives from the perils of the sea, within the United States or upon any American vessel. In 1967 this authority was transferred to the secretary of transportation, with administrative oversight being transferred to the commandant of the U.S. Coast Guard. The Gold Lifesaving Medal, originally designated the "Medal of the First Class," was created for "acts of extreme heroism," while the Silver Lifesaving Medal, designated as "Medal of the Second Class," was for lifesaving acts of a lesser degree of heroism or risk of life.

Civilians as well as military members under certain conditions, are eligible to receive lifesaving medals. Coast Guardsmen may, under certain circumstances, and with the commandant's approval, receive a 10 percent retirement bonus for having been awarded a lifesaving medal. Examples of Coast Guardsmen who have received this bonus are rare because the lifesaving medals are non-military awards, usually reserved for actions that occur during off-duty times.

The medals are among the most valuable, the Gold Medal being comprised of 99.9 percent pure gold, and the Silver Medal being comprised of 99 percent pure silver. The first Gold Lifesaving Medals were awarded in 1876 to three brothers who saved the survivors of a shipwreck on Lake Erie. The brothers maneuvered their twelve-foot boat in high seas and gale-force winds to reach the victims.

The first woman to be awarded the Gold Lifesaving Medal was Ida Lewis, the daughter of the keeper of the Lime Rock Lighthouse in Rhode Island. On February 4, 1881, two soldiers were crossing the ice between the lighthouse and the garrison at Fort Adams when they fell through the weak ice and plunged into the frigid waters below. Miss Lewis, standing on the dangerous ice, threw the survivors a rope and pulled them to safety one at a time. Miss Lewis was known to have rescued at least thirteen others from drowning prior to this incident and as many as twenty-five throughout her career as a light keeper at Lime Rock Light.

Notable recipients of the awards include Navy Commander Chester W. Nimitz, who received the Silver Lifesaving Medal for rescuing a shipmate off Hampton Roads, Virginia, in 1912, and Navy Lieutenant Richard E. Byrd, who also received the Silver Lifesaving Medal for rescuing a shipmate in Santo Domingo in 1914

There is no statute of limitations for the awarding of the Gold or Silver Lifesaving Medals. Take the Pea Island, North Carolina Lifesaving Station, the only all-African American crew in the U.S. Lifesaving Service (the USCG's predecessor organization). The crew was recognized on October 11, 1996, for its daring rescue of the schooner *E.S. Newman*'s crew on October 11, 1896! Relatives of the seven-man Pea Island crew were on hand to see their descendants receive posthumous recognition for having successfully battled hurricane-force winds and the Atlantic's surging waters to save nine men from the *E.S. Newman*.

In a more typical example, the Coast Guard took twelve years to recognize another hero. On the afternoon of July 3, 1984, fisherman Jack Newick rescued Mr. James Sanborn and Mrs. Marjorie Blair from beneath a capsized twenty-seven-foot-long sailing vessel in Little Bay, New Hampshire. Mrs. Blair and Mr. Sanborn were two of a sailboat's crew of five that had been beset by a sudden sixty-knot squall. The other three lucky crew had been literally ejected from the sailboat as it turned turtle and had been rescued by a cruising USCG Auxiliary craft. Mr. Newick, a Mr. Heaphy and a Mr. Scritchfield heard the distress calls issued by the local marina. Newick and his two friends embarked immediately in their fishing boat and were on scene within minutes of the sailboat capsizing. Despite the sixty-six-degree water temperature in Little Bay, Newick jumped in the water and got on top of the capsized sailboat, where he heard Mrs. Blair's desperate cries for help. Mrs. Blair was pounding urgently on the hull with a fire extinguisher, and Newick felt the vibrations through his feet.

On Newick's first dive eighteen feet beneath the surface, he became entangled in the sailboat's rigging, but still managed to determine there were two survivors under the boat. Newick again dove beneath the surface and fastened a line to the lower part of the mast. Mrs. Blair later indicated she and Mr. Sanborn shared a pitch-black, claustrophobic air pocket the length and width of two heads! Time was running out. Heaphy then heaved around on the fishing vessel's winch and righted the sail vessel to a forty-five-degree angle, but did not break the air pocket, which the two victims relied upon. Newick then dove two more times through the maze of rigging and sail, without a wet suit or scuba gear, and brought Mr. Sanborn and Mrs. Blair to the surface. Newick was in the frigid water for twenty-five minutes.

Mrs. Blair was treated at a nearby hospital and released the day after the rescue. The seventy-six-year-old Mr. Sanborn, exhausted from his ordeal, was hospitalized in critical condition. Despite Scritchfield's performance of lifesaving CPR on the boat ride to shore, Sanborn had a stroke two days later and died.

Mrs. Blair still sends her rescuers a Christmas card each year, thanking them for giving her the gift of life. Jack Newick was awarded the Gold Lifesaving Medal in a ceremony at Base South Portland, Maine, in 1996. Heaphy and Scritchfield were also recognized for their extraordinary efforts and received USCG Public Service Commendations.

Recognizing today's and yesterday's heroes is the right thing to do, but can be time consuming, especially as the Coast Guard streamlines itself. While the Coast Guard receives outstanding press coverage when it recognizes old and new acts of courage, that same press coverage routinely brings the promise of one or two new disclosures of unrecognized heroes and heroic acts.

Each disclosure must be researched and investigated, taking typically well over one hundred hours. In the case of older events, where memories have faded and witnesses are not easily located, the time investment is often greater. Many investigators do their research in front of a microfiche reader or sifting through stacks of old papers. Some older events have occurred before the newspapers had converted to computer storage methods. In an environment where the Coast Guard is streamlining, this time investment can be a consideration for the small Search and Rescue units that normally receive these inquiries. However, the USCG must be *semper paratus* (always ready) to recognize its deserving lifesavers lest they sink into oblivion.

Chapter Ten

The Birth of Rescue Boats

By John Galluzzo

Launching a search-and-rescue mission in high, storm-swept seas that could dwarf and topple a small boat seems an impossible, foolish task to some. To Coast Guardsmen and women, however, rescue missions are merely a call to duty, a code of honor and respect. Those time-honored values were indeed present in the Coast Guardsmen of the 1950s, the surfmen of the U.S. Life-Saving Service in the 1870s and the volunteer lifesavers of the Humane Society of the Commonwealth of Massachusetts in the 1840s.

The idea of building and equipping boats to rescue the mariners on those ships in times of trouble is a relatively new phenomenon in human history. Lionel Lukin, an English stagecoach builder, experimented with many of the details that would become staples in lifeboat design for the next century and a half when he developed his first lifeboat in 1784. Taking a twenty-foot Norwegian yawl and fitting it with such stability-enhancing features as a false iron keel for added weight and self-righting capability after rolling and watertight compartments for buoyancy, Lukin developed a boat that would remain upright and maneuverable in rough seas.

Adaptations by shipwrights William Wouldhave and Henry Greathead led to the deployment of a working lifeboat on the mouth of the Tyne by 1790.

The young United States entered the world of organized lifesaving of mariners in distress at sea around the same time when the Humane Society of the Commonwealth of Massachusetts was formed in 1786. Early efforts focused on providing succor for washed ashore shipwreck victims through construction and stocking of houses of refuge along the Massachusetts shore.

The first American lifeboat came later, to Cohasset, Massachusetts, in 1807. Built on Nantucket and shipped to Boston's South Shore for service to the volunteers of the Humane Society, the vessel remained active for about a decade but fell into disrepair at a time when American shipping was at a low point.

The Embargo Act of 1807, prohibiting American trade (meant to harm British trade in particular) and the disruption of regular merchant activity by the Royal Navy during the War of 1812, created a rare era when the need for lifeboats in America was almost nonexistent. Without sailing ships regularly moving from port to port, lifeboats had no raison d'être.

As America moved beyond its infantile struggles and trade increased, the need for lifeboats returned, expanded, and intensified. The Humane Society set upon an ambitious boatbuilding schedule in the 1840s, with their efforts finally being affirmed by the federal government late in the decade in the form of a $5,000 Congressional appropriation for "surfboats, rockets and carronades" to be placed along the New Jersey shore.

In 1871 the new United States Life-Saving Service increased its range and placed additional surfboats and lifeboats ashore near treacherous rips, shoals, rocks and other menaces to safe navigation. In 1899 the service experimented with its first motorized lifeboats on Lake Superior, and mustered the vessels into widespread use by the end of the next decade. Although the marriage then was simply using an existing thirty-four-foot pulling boat from the New Jersey shore, and a two-cylinder, twelve-horsepower engine from the Lake Shore Engine Company of Marquette, Michigan, it forever changed the world of organized maritime search and rescue in America.

The *36500* owed a debt of gratitude to the Life-Saving Service's boat designers of the nineteenth century. And the Life-Saving Service owed a debt of thankfulness to boat designers of the Royal National Lifeboat Institution, England's all volunteer lifesaving organization.

The U.S. Life-Saving Service imported a thirty-foot pulling and sailing lifeboat from across the Atlantic for study in 1873. This became the foundation for future American-made designs. The sleek, elegant, elliptical line of the profile of the *36500* could first be seen in the British boat, and then in the American pulling boats of the 1880s, carried on through the motor lifeboats of the early twentieth century.

By 1920, five years after the merger of the Life-Saving Service and the Revenue Cutter Service that created the Coast Guard, many of the thirty-four-foot and thirty-six-foot motor lifeboats (the latter purposely built as motor lifeboats and categorized as "Type E" for "early") developed early in the century were still in service.

Engines had advanced from twelve horsepower in 1899 to thirty-five to forty horsepower by 1909. Boats of the "H" type of thirty-six-foot motor lifeboat (the "H" only in place because the two men in charge of its development had last names starting with that letter) built after the merger still carried masts and sails for power failure emergencies, problems that plagued the early boats.

In 1920 the Board of Life-Saving Appliances, the Coast Guard's review board for equipment innovation and upgrades, concluded that the boats in service were satisfactory, yet should be retrofitted with new engines and communication technology as they became available. In addition, members firmly believed that thirty-six feet was the maximum length of a motorized lifeboat.

Still the Coast Guard looked toward the future. In June 1928—in a year which had already claimed the lives of three Coast Guardsmen from Manomet Point Coast Guard

Chatham Lifesaving Station. *Courtesy of John J. Galluzzo.*

Station in Plymouth, Massachusetts, when their wooden pulling surfboat pitch-poled near shore following a routine rescue mission—Commandant Frederick C. Billard traveled to Europe to inspect foreign lifeboat designs at the International Congress of Maritime Coast Life-Saving in Paris.

Following tours of lifeboat stations in France, England, Holland and Germany, according to historian Robert Erwin Johnson in *Guardians of the Sea: History of the United States Coast Guard from 1915 to Present*, "Admiral Billard and his associates concluded that their service's equipment was generally superior to that of the European stations."

Billard called for a panel of officers of the service to review information gathered on his trip, and to discuss potential changes to the country's fleet of search-and-rescue craft. The panel recommended the design and construction of a fifty-foot gasoline-powered boat, and if that proved to be unreasonable financially or otherwise, a forty-five-foot boat. According to Johnson, "The district commanders thought that a more powerful version of the 'excellent, able' 36-footer should be built as well."

A year later, the Coast Guard unveiled the type T thirty-six-foot motor lifeboat. Side-by-side comparisons of the types E, H and T boats showed a gradual development away from the classic look and feel of a standard nineteenth-century pulling lifeboat while keeping the aforementioned basic profile. The Type E boat featured a stern engine compartment and a long, open midsection in which, as noted by Ralph Shanks in *The*

U.S. Life-Saving Service: Heroes, Rescues and Architecture of the Early Coast Guard, surfmen often sat facing the stern of the craft, as they would have when rowing a lifeboat. The Type-H boats broke up the open area by placing an engine and steering block just aft of amidships. The types T, TR ("T-Revised," 1931) and TRS ("T-Revised and Simplified," 1937) continued that line of progression.

The *36500*, manufactured at the Coast Guard yard in Curtis Bay, Maryland, in 1946 (the same year that Bernie Webber entered the Coast Guard), fell into the Type TRS category, in the middle of the boat's production run. The major change between the types TR and TRS boats concerned the development of engines reliable enough that the boats came off the line in 1937 without provisions for auxiliary wind propulsion.

The boat that became the backbone of America's lifeboat stations measured thirty-six feet, eight inches in length, and ten feet nine inches in beam. It drafted less than four feet of water, making it available for rescues close to the shore without much fear of grounding. Its single ninety- to one-hundred-horsepower Kermath or Sterling Petrel gasoline engine pushed it at a maximum sustained speed of nine knots for a range of about two hundred nautical miles. Crewed by three, it could take on twenty survivors.

Most importantly, the thirty-six-foot motor lifeboat of the 1930s, 1940s and 1950s was rugged and durable. Coast Guardsmen swore by them, even when confronted with the switch to the technologically advanced forty-four-foot motor lifeboat in the 1960s. Motor lifeboat historian Don Nelson sums up the boat's performance on his webpage dedicated to the history of American lifeboats:

> It was the boat of choice when any emergency arose—no matter how fierce the winds or waves would be…It was self-righting, self-bailing, and unsinkable. The pilot (coxswain) location aft gave good vision for rescue operations and also a better ride in rough seas. Its large power propeller and big rudder allowed quick response and control during tight rescues. The controls were handy and simple. On the down side, besides being relatively slow, the engine exhaust ports were outside below the rear pilot station well. This was noisy and at times exhaust fumes filtered in. It could take almost anything Mother Nature could throw at it. The crewmen would take a beating, but they had the security of this boat. History has recorded countless stories of valiant rescues performed, lives saved that surely would have been lost if not for this boat and its crew…These old woodies out-performed what the designers had planned for them…it will probably go down in history as the most heroic of all MLBs. When they went out, they came back.

As historian Dennis L. Noble notes in *Rescued by the U.S. Coast Guard: Great Acts of Heroism Since 1878*, there is one thing even more imperative for a lifeboat than making it home in one piece. It has to be a tool that the lifeboatmen themselves can trust with their own lives. "Most important, the thirty-six-footer did exactly what it was supposed to do: take generations of U.S. Coast Guardsmen out into gale-swept seas and bring them back safely." Only on rare occasions under the most extreme conditions did thirty-six-footers not return to the ports from which they had headed seaward.

By 1952 the thirty-six-foot motor lifeboat had cemented its legacy as perhaps the greatest small rescue craft ever developed in the United States. On Friday, May 7, 1937, Bosun Hilman J. Persson of the Gray's Harbor Lifeboat Station in Washington gathered a crew to respond to a wreck of a lumber schooner south of the harbor on the rolling Pacific. Persson and his crew left the station at 8:30 p.m. in a sixty-mile-per-hour wind but did not find the ship they were after, the *Trinidad*, until 3:00 a.m. As related by historian James A. Gibbs, in *Pacific Graveyard*, "for fourteen miles, lifeboat *3829* battled walls of water, shaking herself like a wet poodle and going back for more."

When Persson and his men finally pulled alongside the vessel at 5:00 a.m., they found themselves faced with a near-impossible rescue. One sailor later related his thoughts to the *Aberdeen World*:

> *It didn't look like we would get away alive, then just about daylight the Coast Guard began working in…and were we glad to see 'em. I don't believe I ever lived a happier moment in my life than that, when they came up under the lee side. Captain Persson was hanging on with one hand and waving directions with the other. The boat would rise up on a sea and then plunge down in the trough…I was afraid sometimes they never could come up again but the boat would bounce up like a cork, and kept inching in closer. To this hour I don't see how they made it. They would claw their way up to the* Trinidad, *take off a couple of men and then the sea and wind would beat them away. They would haul around and pitch and roll their way back again and take off two or three more men. We almost prayed for them. They could sure take it and come back for more. And it wasn't only the sea…there was rigging and gear plunging around, masts swaying, loading booms, lumbers, and any minute that fore deckload was due to go…but they didn't pay much attention to it…which was plenty lucky for us. Those guys got plenty of guys, take it from me. I'll praise them 'til my last day.*

For rescuing twenty-one crewmen from the wreck of the *Trinidad*, Hilman Persson, Motor Mechanics Roy I. Anderson and Jesse W. Mathews and Surfmen Roy N. Woods and Daniel Hamalainen (on his first search and rescue case) earned the Gold Lifesaving Medal, the United States' highest award for the rescue of life from danger at sea.

In another instance, borne of the global conflict of World War II, a thirty-six-foot motor lifeboat crew rescued eleven survivors of the U-boat torpedoed the *John D. Gill* off North Carolina. Sometimes, as in the case of the torpedoed tanker *Persephone* on May 26, 1942, off the New Jersey coast, a thirty-six-foot motor lifeboat could respond to save the life of just one sailor. However, Coast Guardsmen were always willing to challenge the thirty-six-foot motor lifeboat to hold just one more.

Warrant Officer Garner J. Churchill piloted his thirty-six-foot motor lifeboat out of Humboldt Bay, California, one day in 1931 to rescue the crew of the steam schooner *Cleone*, and found himself in a tight spot. According to historian Ralph Shanks in *Wreck & Rescue Journal*, "When Churchill and his men reached the sinking ship they encountered huge waves and a sea full of 30-foot long bridge timbers that had been the *Cleone*'s deck load." Heavier at one end, the timbers would float vertically, plunge down deeply and then rocket out of the water at unexpected places, falling over horizontally, before repeating the process.

"If even one came up under [the lifeboat]," Churchill told Shanks, "I'd have been a goner."

Churchill moved through the minefield of timbers and successfully removed every sailor from the *Cleone*. "His lifeboat now had so many people in it," wrote Shanks, that it was so low in the water it was barely afloat." Churchill somehow got the sailors—and his own crew—home safely. When asked by Shanks years later how many people he thought he could get into a thirty-six-foot motor lifeboat, Churchill paused and said, "I never found out."

When Bernie Webber, Andy Fitzgerald, Ervin Maske and Richard Livesey headed out to sea on the night of February 18, 1952, to rescue the crew of the *Pendleton*, they had at their command the best lifeboat the Coast Guard had ever developed. The storm-tested type TRS thirty-six-foot motor lifeboat, a vessel with a proven pedigree and decades of proud history, but rarely in conditions the Chatham crewmen were about to face.

Although Bernie Webber may be keenly identified with the *36500*, in November 1961 Bernie was enlisted to evaluate the Coast Guard's newest design, a forty-four-foot motor lifeboat. During the six-week trip, Bernie and his crew stopped at every Coast Guard station from Curtis Bay, Maryland, to Cape Hatteras to the south, then north to Rockland, Maine, and then home to Chatham. "In November and December the boat was tested daily under the most severe weather conditions available at the time," he added. Bernie said the new forty-four was nothing like the *36500*. "She had two heated compartments for survivors, with settees and seat belts to hold them safely in during a rough passage," Webber said. New electronics were part of the package. "She was equipped with radar, direction finding equipment, and several radios with various range and frequencies." The prototype *CG44300* was kept at Chatham for one year while tests continued. The vessel received further testing in Oregon and eventually the forty-four series replaced the thirty-six-foot motor lifeboats, including the *36500*.

Chapter Eleven

Chatham and the Earliest Lifesavers

By John Galluzzo

Chatham's link to Coast Guard history dates to days before Bernie Webber and the *36500* and before motor lifeboats in America changed the way people in distress were rescued.

The first lifesavers who worked along the shore were local men who fished when the seas allowed them, and then risked their lives voluntarily to save sailors in distress when the sea turned angry.

While organized lifesaving of mariners in distress at sea was a centuries-old concept when the American Revolution ended, no system for such work existed in the New World until the middle of the 1780s. A gathering of merchants, philanthropists, doctors and other interested individuals met at the Bunch of Grapes Tavern in Boston to consider the formation of a society dedicated to the restoration of life to the "apparently drowned" in 1786. The next year, the group, by then collectively known as the Humane Society of the Commonwealth of Massachusetts, took their first active, charitable step in placing three small "houses of refuge" on beaches near Boston: one on Lovell's Island, one on Hull's Nantasket Beach and one below Third Cliff in Scituate.

The society became active on Cape Cod almost immediately, advocating for the construction of a lighthouse at Truro and then placing its seventh house of refuge at the head of Stout's Creek in that town in 1792.

Within ten years, that small building that was stocked with emergency supplies for shipwrecked sailors including blankets, firewood and matches washed away during a tidal surge. In 1802 the Society replaced it, erecting similar structures near Peaked Hill Bars in Truro, at Nauset Beach in Eastham, between Nauset and Chatham Harbors and "one on the beach of Cape Malebarre on the sandy of Chatham." When naturalist Henry David Thoreau visited such a building on the Lower Cape during his jaunts that made up the text for his posthumously published *Cape Cod*, he decried the broken down shack as a poor attempt at charity, while a companion corrected him by saying that for humanity, it instead was a good start.

The Humane Society became interested in lifeboats in 1807, placing the first one in Cohasset that year, but eventually letting it deteriorate into useless condition. It took a series of tragic December storms, known as the Triple Hurricanes of 1839—which left Cape Cod towns saddled with the care of hundreds of widows and orphans of drowned fishermen caught in the storms—to spur the society into new action. A Cape Cod man and the ninth president of the Humane Society, Benjamin Rich of Truro, put a plan into motion. By pressuring the state of Massachusetts to examine its role in the saving of lives from shipwreck, Rich drove forward the concept to have lifeboats constructed and placed in eighteen volunteer-maintained boathouses from the North Shore's Plum Island to Martha's Vineyard by 1845. By the time of the country's centennial celebration in 1876, Massachusetts boasted sixty volunteer lifeboat crews.

By 1848, the federal government caught on to what Massachusetts's philanthropists were accomplishing. That year, Congress appropriated $5,000 for the purchase of "surfboats, rockets and carronades" for placement along the approaches to New York Harbor, line-throwing guns by then becoming standard tools in the race to save shipwrecked mariners.

The appropriation signaled the birth of the United States Life-Saving Service, a predecessor of the modern United States Coast Guard. The Life-Saving Service came to Cape Cod in 1872, after a horrific series of winter storms forced the government to re-examine its efforts to build a network of lifesaving stations along the East Coast. A Maine man, Sumner Increase Kimball, took over as the service's first and only general superintendent, and turned an ineffective collection of stations manned with political appointees, and men afraid to even row their boats to shipwrecks into a world-renowned system of efficient, well-trained "storm warriors."

Kimball examined the coastline and immediately designated those places that deserved new station construction as priorities. The fact that Cape Cod towns saw nine stations erected in the first year alone signified the dangers to sailors rounding the Cape between Boston and New York; that Chatham saw two stations constructed in that first year solidified its reputation as a shipwreck hotbed. Unfortunately, time would prove that two stations were not enough to watch over the changing sands and bars of the extreme south end of Cape Cod.

Both the Chatham Life-Saving Station and the Monomoy Life-Saving Station served seafarers both local and visiting alike. The Chatham station sat, originally, at the northern end of then–Monomoy Island, "within easy distance of Chatham village," according to J.W. Dalton, author of *The Life-Savers of Cape Cod*. In 1880, when erosion threatened to destroy the station at its current site, the service moved the station north to protect the mouth of Old Harbor. A move back to its original site a few years later prompted locals to believe that a new station would soon be built at Old Harbor, but it took a major shipwreck on the Old Harbor Bars, that of the *Calvin B. Orcutt* in 1896, to push the service to add the third station to Chatham's shores.

The Monomoy Life-Saving Station called for a stouter "surfman," as the patrolmen of the service were called, one who could stand a bit more isolation than his brethren serving at stations near the hearts of other communities. Located about two-thirds of the

The old Station Chatham, 1942. *Courtesy of John J. Galluzzo.*

way down the eastern side of Monomoy, the station stood sentinel over Shovelful and Handkerchief Shoals and the busy waters of Nantucket Sound. Most of the men, if not all, hailed from nearby Harwich. After construction of the new Monomoy Point Life-Saving Station abreast of the "Powder Hole" at the southern end of the island in 1902, word floated around Chatham that the old Monomoy station would soon be closed.

Fate, through a verdict rendered by Mother Nature, delivered a message to the Life-Saving Service that downsizing on Cape Cod would not advisable.

The Monomoy Disaster
By Theresa M. Barbo
Originally published in The Cape Cod Voice *with the title "Harwich Buries Seven Husbands"*

Isaac Thomas Foye—a lifesaver stationed at Monomoy—awoke to cold and rain the morning of March 12, 1902.

He was young, and so good looking the local girls voted him "the handsome surfman." And he was doomed.

Momomoy keeper Marshall Eldredge ordered Foye to don storm clothes and head out a half mile to Shovelful Shove to rescue the crew of the coal barge Wadena, *lodged there since March 11 during a ferocious northeast gale. The* Wadena *was one of two coal barges being towed to Boston by the tug* Sweepstakes. *The other, the* John C. Fitzpatrick, *was stranded nearby. The plan was to refloat the barges when the weather broke.*

Eldredge thought the Wadena *was empty, but the tug captain told him there were men on board and when he walked to the point for a closer look, he saw the vessel flying an American flag upside down.*

Aerial view of Station Chatham. *Courtesy of John J. Galluzzo.*

"We must go! There is a distress flag in the rigging!" he was heard to say.

Young Foy never worked alone. Five other lifesavers—all Harwich men—quickly changed into regulation gear: flannel shirts, khaki pants, oilcloths and boots. Elijah Kendrick and Osborne Chase were on duty too, as was Edgar C. Small. Valentine Nickerson, a tall, experienced seaman would join the rescue team along with Arthur Rogers.

The lifesavers were led by Seth Linwood Ellis, Monomoy's number one surfman.

By 1902, the U.S. Life-Saving Service—ancestor to today's Coast Guard—had been around for thirty years. On Cape Cod, 13 stations were manned by no fewer than 120 men. There were about 32 stations along the Massachusetts coast. Lifesavers had rescued 217 people on 28 vessels between August 8, 1901, and June 3, 1902. [Some thirty-six other ships of varying size and tonnage avoided potential tragedy, warned off the dangerous shoals by signals put out by patrolling Lifesavers. That very year—1902—Congress had approved a funding package of $1,742,000 for the U.S. Life-Saving Service across the nation.]

The tragedy to unfold within hours would be remembered by Cape Codders as the most horrific day in Massachusetts lifesaving history.

Noontime. It took all morning for Seth, Edgar, Elijah, Thomas and Keeper Eldredge, who joined the rescue party as the surfboat left shore, to reach the stranded Wadena.

All that time, five stranded men scared out of their wits watched from the barge as the gallant rescue party painstakingly and methodically rowed toward the lee side of the Wadena. One by one, the five men lowered themselves down a line thrown up toward the deck: barge owner William Mack, Captain Christian Olsen of Boston, and three Portuguese sailors, Walter Zeved, Robert Malanox, and Manuel Enos.

For a moment, it seemed like a successful rescue. Then a huge wave shoved the surfboat away from the protective lee of the barge and into the grip of high seas. Panicked, the men of the Wadena *grabbed onto their rescuers, whose now entangled arms could no longer row and control the boat. Twice the surfboat capsized and twice was righted, only to be knocked over again.*

Thirteen men clung to the overturned boat and one by one, the five from the barge were pulled to their deaths.

Eight lifesavers clung to the overturned surfboat. Osborne Chase, the father of three daughters, was the first to sink out of sight. Keeper Eldredge—a father of three—a strong and capable surfman, was next. Elijah Kendrick, an excellent swimmer and father of two, became entangled in a loose sail and was pulled under. Five men were left as the thundering sea crashed in their ears.

Quickly three more lost their grips: Valentine Nickerson, father of four daughters, Edgar Small, with two children, and the handsome Foye. Arthur Rogers, exhausted beyond comprehension, was carried away by a wave. Only Ellis remained, but barely. On the other stranded coal barge nearby, Chatham mariner Elmer Mayo, a captain helping with the salvage, saw the drifting, capsized surfboat nearing the John C. Fitzpatrick. *Captain Mayo lowered a dory and hit the waves, determined to save the lifesaver. Fighting exhaustion and fright, Seth Ellis reached for Captain Mayo's extended oar and held on for dear life. He struggled aboard the small dory and the pair headed for shore.*

Within days, Ellis, now acting keeper, took to the water again and rescued the crew of the schooner Elwood Burton, *stranded on Hankerchief Shoal, while Harwich prepared to bury the husbands of seven women and fathers to 15 children.*

For the rest of his life, Elmer Mayo of Chatham was celebrated as a hero for his rescue of Ellis.

After nearly perishing together, both went on to live long lives, passing on, ironically, in the same year—1935.

The Humane Society of the Commonwealth of Massachusetts set out into the streets to raise funds for the widows and orphans, delivering $50,000 for their comfort. The United States Life-Saving Service decided not to close the Monomoy station after all.

The Life-Saving Service indeed paid homage to the lifesavers and tribute to the treacherous offshore waters of the Cape by designing and building boats designed to handle rough surf, the Monomoy and Race Point class surfboats. The former carried the name of the disaster that killed nearly an entire crew wherever it was shipped for service.

With technological advances in both communication and in lifeboat design—specifically the addition of motors to small rescue craft—and the opening of the Cape Cod Canal in 1914, the need for a heavy Life-Saving Service presence on the sandy stretch from Chatham to Provincetown diminished considerably. When President William Howard Taft urged "unifunctionalism" within the federal government, the Life-Saving Service merged with the Revenue Cutter Service to form the Coast Guard. More consolidation of assets took place in the years to come.

With the passage of the National Prohibition Act of 1919—known as the Volstead Act for the Minnesota Republican who sponsored the measure—Coast Guardsmen, once known as "heroes of the surf," became public enemies overnight to anyone who wanted a nip of drink from time to time.

The men, who had joined the service to "save lives and property," as the old mantra went, now found themselves tasked with arresting friends and countrymen for the smuggling of spirits. Author Henry Beston did his best to romanticize the life of the patrolling surfman—who was still walking the beaches at night with a kerosene lantern in hand in 1928, as had his fellow lifesavers before him in 1872—in *The Outermost House*, but it would take more than that to heal the wounds of the "noble experiment" with a dry America.

World War II, surprisingly, did much to reinvent the image of the modern Coast Guardsman. After the war, only three Coast Guard stations remained where once thirteen protected the Lower Cape: Race Point in Provincetown, Nauset in Eastham and one in Chatham. Ironically, in the town in America that had more lifesaving stations than any other community, those four buildings were bypassed in favor of the quarters of the old Chatham lighthouse keeper's dwelling. Built in 1877 on an eroding shoreline at that moment set to claim an earlier set of lights, the twin Chatham lighthouse towers guided mariners into Chatham Harbor and helped set courses up or down the coast. One lighthouse was removed in 1923 to Nauset Beach, leaving its twin behind. When the Coast Guard moved permanently into the keeper's quarters, it expanded the building for crew and office space setting up a home for years to come.

The town of Chatham, too, was changing. Although much of the Cape remained primarily as Henry David Thoreau had seen it in the middle of the previous century, with dirt roads leading past scrub pines to sandy beaches, postwar America was learning to love the automobile and its alluring access to adventure on the open road. New age explorers were looking for novel places to live, work and play. Cape Cod was being "discovered," and in Chatham, zoning regulations became the new buzzwords among selectmen.

When Bernie Webber and his fellow crewman reported to the Chatham station for the first time, they would have seen the spire William Mack erected in memory of the Monomoy disaster of March 17, 1902. Each day when they went to work, it stood as a reminder of what could happen offshore even in times when the sea appeared calm.

Chatham Bar "was rougher than hell," Joe Nickerson of Chatham said several years ago when asked about that night. Nickerson was a tenth generation Cape Codder and knew what he was talking about, so the crew of the *36500* had grave cause for concern.

Chatham's tragic past with the sea carried a permanent reminder in that monument.

Chapter Twelve

NEW ENGLAND IN 1952

By John Galluzzo

At 5:55 p.m. on Monday, February 18, 1952, just as Bernie and the *36500* crew set off from the fish pier to attempt to rescue the stranded crew of the *Pendleton*, as was the quintessential American way, New England families sat down to supper. It had been a heck of a couple of days. Snow had blanketed western Massachusetts dropping more than twenty inches of the white stuff in towns around Springfield.

Northfield, Vermont residents watched as 28 inches piled up outside, while residents of Somerset (23.5 inches) and Bloomfield (22 inches) hunkered down for a long wait indoors. In Lewiston, Maine, where on the third Monday of the month, according to the town charter, an election was to be held for the offices of mayor and members of the Board of Aldermen, the snow had stopped the wheels of government cold. The storm, which had intensified during the night, left the streets and sidewalks impassable by 8:00 a.m., the time when the wardens expected to be opening the doors to the more than 21,000 enrolled voters. Instead, they found themselves at home, struggling to get out their front doors. The city clerk tried in vain to even deliver the ballots to the polling places. By 5:55 p.m., not a single vote had been cast.

Dana Eldredge, in *Cape Cod Lucky: In Another Time*, remembered things this way: "By 1952 the Outer Cape was growing up. It had cast its lot with sensible growth as evidenced with the passage of Senator Stone's bill authorizing the two-year community college. Towns were adopting zoning, albeit after much wrangling at the often boisterous town meetings."

Oddly, a touch of late summer had hit the Cape earlier in the month. On February 2, 1952, a tropical depression formed just north of Honduras and began spinning its way north toward Cancun. Turning to the northeast it grazed Cuba, passed over Key West and made landfall near Cape Sable, Florida. Meteorologists in Miami clocked sustained winds at fifty-nine miles per hour and gusts up to sixty-eight miles per hour.

Moving into the Atlantic, the storm strengthened off the coast of South Carolina. The extratropical storm pushed onto Cape Cod and finally eastern Maine on February 5, causing power outages for 15,000 people in the Northeast. It was the first time a tropical cyclone had formed in the Atlantic in February. The storm followed a severe January winter storm that stranded the Orleans High School basketball team on Nantucket Island for five days until the seas calmed enough to let them pass back home.

On February 18, 1952, at 5:55 p.m., according to Dana Eldredge, "The rotary near the Hyannis Airport was plowed one lane wide. The snow was well over the road signs. Giant rotary plows from Maine were brought in to clear the roads."

Out at sea, the crews of the T-2-type tankers *Fort Mercer* and *Pendleton* were in serious trouble. In Portland, Maine, the Coast Guard cutter *Acushnet* stood by for orders, expecting to be deployed to the scene of one or both ships. "And so ran the vein of scuttlebutt aboard the broad-beamed, black and grey sea-going tug CGC *Acushnet* (WAT167)," said Coast Guardsman Sid Morris in *Sea Classics* magazine years later,

> *that frigid, snow packed morning of 18 February 1952. The snow emerged violently from the cloud-bulged skies the morning before, but since this was February in Portland, Maine, I had come to regard the message of nature as a regularly scheduled event.*
>
> *The icy, biting wind swept in at noon and by dusk, their velocity had built up to 35 knots. That night the big black ship surged and rolled at the end of the Maine State Pier as if she were bucking thirty foot swells.*

The CGC *Cook Inlet*, also at Portland on February 18, 1952, headed to sea for ocean weather station duty. Young Seaman Frederick G. "Bud" Cooney remembered in *Wreck & Rescue Journal* that

> *the gangway, our only bridge to shore, was hauled aboard and lashed secure. Light snow began whipping about in a gusty wind…A couple of seamen from the cutter* Acushnet, *tied up aft of us, were stationed at the bollards to handle the mooring lines. They soon became aware that the number 2 line and the bow line were frozen solid to the pier, and would have to be cut when we were letting go. Fire axes were provided to accomplish this task.*

For Cooney, a recent graduate of Coast Guard boot camp in Cape May, New Jersey, February 18, 1952, would be his first day underway as a member of the Coast Guard.

Weather aside, what was the world and its culture like in 1952?

Many folks in New England and the rest of the country, for that matter, planned a night in front of the television. Two shows in particular warranted plenty of attention. Lucille Ball and Desi Arnaz promised a half hour of laughter in the new episode of their five-month-old program, *I Love Lucy*.

George Burns and Gracie Allen planned to have Mr. and Mrs. America in stitches as well. The hilarity all would revolve around the premise of Gracie taking a tumble in a department store, and the nervousness of the staff doing their best to make sure that she didn't sue the store.

Television had made major strides in 1951. First, on June 25, in a month in which television manufacturer RCA launched its color system, CBS presented the first color television program, starring Arthur Godfrey, Ed Sullivan and Faye Emerson. A little more than a month later, on August 11, the Boston Braves and the Brooklyn Dodgers battled it out in a doubleheader in the first sporting event ever televised in color. Red Barber made the call with Connie Desmond as the Dodgers, behind Ralph Branca, took the first game in a rout, 8–1. The Braves took the second game, 8–4.

On September 22, 1952, Duke University and the University of Pittsburgh competed before the first-ever nationwide TV audience for a sporting event. The World Series, between the New York Giants and the New York Yankees, would be the first one ever broadcast from east to west as well, but not before Bobby Thomson hit the "shot heard round the world," easily the most famous home run of all time. On October 3, 1951, with two runners on and two outs in the bottom of the ninth inning, Thomson slammed a pitch to left off Dodgers pitcher Ralph Branca that cleared the fence and gave the Giants the National League pennant. With just 49 games to go on August 11, the day of the first game televised in color, the Dodgers had held a 13½-game lead in the National League. With one swing of the bat, the Dodgers' season was over, and the Giants were off to face the Yankees in the World Series.

On February 18, 1952, Boston sports fans had only one entertainment choice. The Bruins, led by Milt Schmidt and Johnny Pierson, skated into Detroit that night to face the Red Wings. Had the game been scheduled for the Boston Garden, it would most likely have been postponed. Nevertheless, since the game was in Detroit, fans could tune into WHDH radio to listen for the call from Frank Ryan and Leo Egan.

The Red Sox, of course, would not be playing in February, but would be looking forward to spring training in March in Sarasota, Florida. The previous year's campaign had been an encouraging one, as the hard luck Sox—who had lost the 1946 World Series to the Cardinals, a one-game playoff to the Cleveland Indians in 1948 and had come in a heartbreaking second to the Yankees by a single game in 1949—gritted out a third place finish. But the news out of Fenway Park was not so good early in the year. Ted Williams, the Red Sox's slugging left fielder, who with second baseman Bobby Doerr, shortstop Johnny Pesky and center fielder Dom DiMaggio had formed the heart of the Red Sox line-up (Doerr retired at the end of the 1951 season) made a grim announcement. With the war heating up in Korea, he knew it was time he got into the fight. The Marine Corps Reserves called the World War II veteran back to active duty, and by the spring he was training in the F9F Panther for combat overseas. Williams, who had led the American League in slugging percentage, on-base percentage, total bases and bases on balls in 1951, hoped to be leading the Korean Theater of Operations in downed MiGs by the end of the year.

The war in Korea, in fact, had the nation's spirits down. Peace talks had begun during the summer of 1951, but had stalled. The war itself was being fought for a new, hard-to-grasp concept—that of "containment" of Communism, the theory of keeping that political form of government as far from the United States as possible. Although the heaviest fighting had taken place during the first year of the war, Americans were still being killed on a seemingly daily basis in the far-off land. On Sunday, February 10, one of the few heroes of the war on the American side met his untimely end. Major George A. Davis Jr., 334th Fighter Squadron, 4th Fighter Group, 5th Air Force, died after notching his thirteenth and fourteenth downed Communist MiG jets. Trying to intercept a third jet before it jumped other American planes, Davis's F86 Sabre suddenly shuddered with jolts from gunfire on the ground. His plane spun out of control and crash-landed behind enemy lines, taking the life of the country's greatest jet-age ace. On Monday, February 18, 1952, the California National Guard's 224th Infantry Regiment lost seven men at Pusan: Private First Class (PFC) Joseph Pavlak, PFC Frank J. Liscombe, First Lieutenant James F. Inglesby, Sergeant Will T. Cross, Sergeant Raymond Mendoza, PFC George F. O'Quinn and PFC Lawrence M. Gold. The 578th Engineer Battalion, also part of California's 40th Infantry Division, lost one man that day, Sergeant William Schoolcraft.

The biggest news out of Korea that day, though, concerned a prisoner of war riot on Koje-Do, an island off the southern end of the Asian nation. A surprising military success at Inchon late in 1951 left U.S. 8th Army forces with an overabundance of prisoners—137,000 or so—and limited space and manpower to contain them. The move to the island quelled some problems, but did not stop others from developing.

The camp was divided into four enclosures housing eight compounds each, and each compound, designed to hold about a thousand men, became jammed with five times the optimum number. Problems developed within the ranks of the prisoners as Communist and anti-Communist factions formed. In the darkness of night, when guards left the prisoners alone, kangaroo courts "tried" and sentenced inmates, often calling for and delivering execution as punishment. Rock fights broke out, leaving dozens dead or injured. Gangs from both sides doled out beatings indiscriminately. Education programs aimed at showing the righteousness of democracy and the evils of Communism agitated Chinese and pro-Communist Korean prisoners, and metal shop classes designed to teach job skills for life after release effectively became home weapons courses.

In January 1952, the prospect of a new wave of screenings targeting the redesignation of many of the prisoners as civilian internees pushed the Communist bloc to the limit. On February 18, 1952, the four companies of the Third Battalion, Twenty-seventh Infantry Regiment made a show of force in Compound 62, a gathering of approximately 5,600 defiant, pro-Communist prisoners, determined to screen them for reclassification. The Americans, with bayonets fixed, divided the prisoners into four groups, but the prisoners struck out with their handmade weapons, rushing out of the barracks with everything from tent poles to axes. The Americans tossed concussion grenades at the more than 1,000 screaming and advancing prisoners, but when that failed, machine guns blared, killing 55 prisoners instantly. Twenty-two died later of wounds received in the melee. One American soldier died and 38 received wounds. On February 18, 1952, the Korean War seemed endless.

President Harry S. Truman knew that the Korean conflict had to be resolved soon or else his presidency would be forever tarnished. But Truman had already dug a deep hole for himself, as his approval rating by the American people was at just 22 percent in the month of February 1952, the lowest ever given any U.S. president.

Truman recorded eight specific thoughts about his role as the political leader of the United States in his diary on February 18, 1952:

> *The President's Duties.*
> 1. *By the Constitution, he is the Executive of the Government.*
> 2. *By the Constitution, he is the Commander in Chief of the Armed Forces.*
> 3. *By the Constitution, he is the responsible head of Foreign Policy and with the help of his Secretary of State implements foreign policy.*
> 4. *He is the leader of his Party, makes and carries out the Party Platform as best he can.*
> 5. *He is the Social Head of the State. He entertains visiting Heads of State.*
> 6. *He is the No. 1 public relations man of the Government. He spends a lot of time persuading people to do what they should do without persuasion.*
> 7. *He has more duties and powers than a Roman Emperor, a Gen., a Hitler or a Mussolini; but he never uses those powers or prerogatives, because he is a democrat (with a little d) and because he believes in the Magna Carta and the Bill of Rights. But first he believes in the XXth Chapter of Exodus, the Vth Chapter of Deuteronomy, and the V, VI, & VIIth chapters of the Gospel according to St. Matthew.*
> 8. *He should be a Cincinnatus, Marcus Aurelius Antoninus, a Cato, Washington, Jefferson and Jackson all in one. I fear that there is no such man. But if we have one who tries to do what is right because it is right, the greatest Republic in the history of the world will survive.*

Truman obviously felt, after six and a half years as president of the United States that he was not the man who would carry the "greatest Republic in the history of the world" into the future. Although technically qualified to run for another term (Congress passed the Twenty-second Amendment to the Constitution on March 21, 1947, limiting presidents to two elected terms; Truman had taken over as President in April 1945 following the death of Franklin Delano Roosevelt and had been elected to the post in 1948), he decided not to run against Republican Dwight D. Eisenhower in November.

The war on Communism took another provocative step on February 18, 1952. Shortly after the end of the Second World War, much like had happened that day in the Koje-Do prison camp, Communist and non-Communist nations began a staring contest, soon to be known as the Cold War. Fearing that the Soviet Union, now a world power after fighting on the side of the Allies during the war, would try to spread its wings by attacking nearby European countries, many of those seemingly targeted nations formed a new military alliance, the North Atlantic Treaty Organization

The signing of the Treaty of Brussels on March 17, 1948, formed an initial alliance of Belgium, the Netherlands, Luxembourg, France and the United Kingdom, later called the Western European Union, however, American firepower was seen as necessary to truly combat any Soviet threat. On April 4, 1949, the United States and six other countries—Canada, Iceland, Italy, Portugal, Denmark and Norway—added their names to the pact, now known as NATO. On February 18, 1952, the agreement extended to the eastern Mediterranean, as Turkey and Greece pledged their support to their now-brethren nations.

Amid all the political tension still rife throughout the world in the few short years following the cessation of the global conflict, a relatively new world spectacle, the Winter Olympics, began on February 14 as Princess Raghnild of Norway opened the games in Oslo. The games had taken a twelve-year hiatus following the fourth winter Olympiad in Garmisch-Partenkirchen, Germany, in 1936, on the eve of World War II. The eventual invasions of Poland, Austria, France and others postponed the next scheduled games in 1940. No games were held again until the fifth Olympiad in St. Moritz, Switzerland, in 1948. It was obvious there that although the war had ended, the wounds remained open. The U.S. bobsled team had to compete in patched-up sleds, as unknown saboteurs did their best to disable the team's equipment prior to the competition. In an amazing instance of infighting on the American side, two rival amateur hockey organizations sent complete teams to the games, each one claiming the right to do so. The Amateur Athletic Union's team won out, although the Amateur Hockey Association team was allowed to compete in the games, the results of their games did not count.

In the 1952 games, 694 athletes—585 men and 109 women—from thirty nations (including Germany and Japan, participating for the first time since the end of the war) competed in twenty-two events in six sports. An amazing lack of snow put the organizers into fits of anxiety just before the games started, but a last-minute storm saved the day. For the first time, women competed in cross-country skiing, and men and women both tried their hands (and legs) at the giant slalom. American figure skater Dick Buttons, the 1948 gold medal winner in the event, hoped to defend his title, and Norwegian Arnfinn Bergman set out to give the host country its sixth gold medal in the ski jump in six Olympiads.

February 18, 1952, turned out to be the greatest day in the history of Norwegian sports. The country that invented modern alpine skiing claimed two gold medals that morning. Hallgeir Brendan took first honors in the eighteen-kilometer cross-country skiing event, and Simon Slattvik jumped and raced to first place in the Nordic combined. The capper of the day came when Hjalmar Andersen edged out Dutchman Wim van der Voort by two-tenths of a second to take the gold medal in the men's 1500 meters speed skating competition. Workers across the city left their posts and poured into the streets to celebrate.

One country that sent a team to the competition was in need of a huge spiritual lift. As Americans picked through their mail over the weekend and found their February 18, 1952 copy of *Time* magazine, they read of the latest happenings in England. King George VI, the gentle-spirited monarch who lent an air of strength to his British subjects during the darkest days of World War II, had died on February 6, leaving millions to mourn, including Americans.

"About 11 o'clock," said ex-Paratrooper Jack Greagor in Los Angeles, "a guy pulls in for gas. I filled him up and he leaned out and said, 'Did you hear about the King dying?' I knew right then who he meant. Jeez, I was surprised. And kind of stunned. I remember when he inspected us in England. You can't help feeling sorry for the man. The Princess inspected us too, when she was in uniform herself. She just walked down the line in those god-awful brown stockings, just as big as life, and now she's Queen. It sure is a jolt."

Millions of other U.S. citizens felt a jolt, too, at the unexpected news that death had come to George VI, the quiet men who brightened the Crown tarnished by Edward VIII's abdication. Tens of thousands of Americans like Gas Station Attendant Jack Greagor had served in Britain as soldiers and bluejackets; tens of thousands more had visited the British Isles as tourists in the years since. But even those Americans who had never crossed the Atlantic, and never would, knew more about Britain and felt closer to the British than had any other U.S. generation.

This sense of familiarity had come so gradually, and amid so much turmoil, that few had stopped to think much about it before, although in the years since World War II began darkening the earth, U.S. newspapers, radio networks and newsreels had reported the story of Britain more thoroughly than foreign news had ever been reported before. The average American of this decade would have found it hard to name either the Prime Minister of Canada or the President of Mexico, but he knew almost as much about the politics, the economic difficulties and the foreign policy of Great Britain as he did of his own country.

Six black horses drew the caisson carrying King George VI's coffin from the royal summer estate Sandringham in Norfolk, where he died, to the local railroad station for transport to London. The 103-mile journey ended at Westminster Hall, where the King lied in state before the funeral. On Friday, February 15, the British people paid their final respects to the King, as he was buried after funeral services at St. George's Chapel in Windsor Castle.

Upon the King's death on February 6, young Princess Elizabeth became Queen Elizabeth II. Traveling through Kenya on her way to a tour of Australia and New Zealand, she received the news of her father's passing from Prince Philip, with her on the journey. They stayed that night for dinner at the Treetops Hotel in Thika before setting out for home. The following day, heralds announced her ascendancy to the throne from St. James' Palace.

News of the doings in England had dominated dinner table discussions, even in America, for nearly two weeks. *Time* magazine informed one and all that much else had been happening in February 1952, much of it to do with Hollywood. Esther Williams was working on her latest film, about the life story of Annette Kellerman, inventor of the one-piece bathing suit for women. Kellerman, a technical advisor on the set, had been arrested forty-two years previously in Boston for daring to sport the outfit in public. At sixty-two, Charlie Chaplin was just about to finish his latest offering, *Limelight*. Other news in the Troubled Times column reported that

When Jane Russell, Lana Turner, Joan Crawford, Jimmy Durante and Victor Mature failed to appear as witnesses at the trial of a Hollywood fashion designer charged with stealing a fur piece, the court lost its temper, said: "These Hollywood people ask the protection of the courts, but fail to appear when it doesn't suit their convenience. Who do they think they are? Movie people are no better than anyone else."

Although New Englanders were not allowed the luxury of taking in a movie on February 18, 1952, had they been, perhaps they would have checked out the newest film from Paramount's comedy duo of Dean Martin and Jerry Lewis, *Sailor Beware*. *Time*'s reviewer explained the plot, but shied away from giving the film a thumbs-up:

As comedians, Martin & Lewis resemble a two-man Milton Berle. Like Berle, Dean Martin is brashly self-confident, always ready with the knowing leer. Like Berle, Jerry Lewis twists his arms and legs into grotesque positions; his voice alternates between a high, cretinous [sic] whine and a low, idiot mumble; he stares at the camera with crossed eyes and unhinged jaw and, for variety, pantomimes effeminacy.

The film's resemblance to old-time burlesque is underlined by the presence of bosomy Corinne Calvet, and by Marion Marshall and a bevy of girls whose only duty seems to be to chase hysterically after Jerry Lewis.

Time readers also cringed at this grisly tale that weekend:

When the police arrested John Arno Schulz, a 16-year-old Milwaukee high-school boy, for speeding in St. Louis County, Mo. This week, they asked him what he was doing so far from home. He readily told them:

"Saturday night I wanted to go to a basketball game. My mother kept arguing about staying out late...My mother and I have been arguing and fighting ever since I can remember...After dinner I went up into the attic and got my father's .410 shotgun, a bolt-action gun holding four shells...My father had left for La Crosse. I put a handful of shells into my pocket and came down the stairs and put the gun in the hall. Ralph Trede called up. He is 17 years old. He asked me if I was going to the basketball game.

"Then I got into an argument with my mother again...I asked her where the [car] keys were but she wouldn't tell me. I got the gun [and] went back to the kitchen...and called her by her name, Catherine. She turned around...I shot her in the stomach. She fell, started to get up, and I fired another shot, hitting her in the face. About that time my brother Robert, eleven years old, started toward the phone...to call the police. I shot him, and I think I hit him in the shoulder.

"He ran into the bedroom, and my little sister Catherine, six years old, began screaming. Robert was rolling on the floor and trying to get under the bed, and I shot him again. [Catherine] was screaming too much, so I shot her. I was just mad or something. I went back to the kitchen and shot [mother] again. I went back to the bedroom. My brother was moving a little. I reached over the bed and shot him again. I don't know how

many times I shot my sister. I dragged my mother into a bedroom and closed the door. I found the keys to the car in a jewel box on the dresser.

"*I picked up Donald Smith and Everett Myers, and we went to the basketball game at Pulaski High School. Pulaski won, I think it was 55 to 46. After I got home from the basketball game, it was about 1 o'clock in the morning. I took a bath, shaved, put on a new suit and packed, my grip. I looked for money. I gathered up about $127. I wrote a note to my father…It said: 'Sorry things have happened this way. Maybe we will meet again…Your Twisted Son.' Then I drove toward Geneva, Illinois. I followed* [Route] *66.*

"*I had nothing against my brother and sister. They were my buddies. I don't have to go to the funerals, do I?"*

When St. Louis police called them, officers in Milwaukee reported that they had no knowledge of such a murder, but 15 minutes later the boy's story was verified—his father got back to Milwaukee, walked into the house, and all but stumbled over the bodies of his wife and two children.

February 18, 1952, though, would also be remembered as a banner day in the history of crime fighting in America. "Slick Willie" Sutton had committed crimes, escaped, committed more crimes and escaped again in a regular pattern since the 1930s. Also known as "The Actor," Sutton specialized in impersonations to get his bank jobs done, from mailmen to messengers to policemen. He was also known for his politeness during robberies. One person who witnessed one of his thefts likened it to being at the theater with an usher, who just happened to be carrying a gun.

On February 18, Sutton, who had a taste for fine clothing, caught the eye of a tailor's son on the subway in New York City. The FBI, which had him listed as the number three most wanted man in America, had distributed Sutton's image to tailors' shops as well as police departments. The young man followed Sutton, who had escaped from a life sentence in Philadelphia County Prison on February 10, 1947, by impersonating a guard and climbing over the wall on a ladder, to a gas station. He observed Sutton purchasing a car battery, alerted the police and watched as they arrested him one final time.

Regular *Time* readers on Cape Cod already knew that their little corner of the world was becoming more popular as the years went by. Subscription services general manager Ed King informed the editorial staff at the magazine in May 1951 that the Cape towns called for a 700 percent increase in subscription deliveries during the summer months, meaning that readers were hoping to have their magazines follow them on vacation. The locals knew, too, that the current population of about 47,000 permanent residents from Bourne to Provincetown would likely significantly increase in the years to come.

At 5:55 p.m. on February 18, 1952, Coast Guardsmen Bernie Webber, Andy Fitzgerald, Richard Livesey and Ervin Maske dashed their way to the *36500* at Chatham's fish pier, hell-bent on saving the lives of the crew of the *Pendleton* that had survived the splitting of the ship into two pieces.

"Not one of the commercial fishermen who watched the tiny U.S.C.G. thirty-six footer butt its way into those massive, storm driven waves ever expected it to return," said Dana Eldredge. "Later revelations by the crew of the small boat revealed that they, too, didn't really expect to return."

"Until that night, the Coast Guard's reputation was spotty at best. Ever after, their reputation, at least in Chatham, has had a sterling luster."

At 5:55 p.m., on February 18, 1952, the lives of Webber, Fitzgerald, Livesey and Maske had changed forever.

About the Authors

Theresa Mitchell Barbo is the founder and president of the Cape Cod Maritime Research Association, a nonprofit organization that since 1996 has sponsored the annual Cape Cod Maritime History Symposium, a key event of the annual Cape Maritime Days held each May.

As an award-winning former broadcast journalist and history editor at *The Cape Cod Voice*, Theresa has lectured on Cape Cod history and related cultures throughout New England. She is author of *True Accounts of Yankee Grit and Ingenuity: from* The Cape Cod Voice and *The Cape Cod Murder of 1899: The Punishment and Redemption of Edwin Ray Snow*, both published by The History Press.

She holds BA and MA degrees from the University of Massachusetts–Dartmouth and has completed the Executive Integral Leadership Program at the Mendoza College of Business at the University of Notre Dame.

For her work in assisting Captain Webster with the May 2002 Gold Medal Reunion in Chatham, the Coast Guard awarded Theresa its Public Service Commendation Medal.

Theresa is currently Director of the Cape Cod Bay Ocean Sanctuary Program at the Provincetown Center for Coastal Studies. She and her husband, Daniel, reside in Yarmouth Port with their children, Katherine and Thomas.

John Galluzzo is the executive director of the United States Life-Saving Service Heritage Association. He is also editor of their quarterly magazine of Coast Guard history, *Wreck & Rescue Journal*. John is a plank-owning and honorary life member of the Foundation for Coast Guard History, a coauthor of the foundation's book *The Coast Guard* and the executive director of the Cape Cod Maritime Research Association. This is his fifth book with The History Press.

John holds a BA in history from University of Massachusetts–Amherst and is a graduate of the Munson Institute of Maritime Studies at Mystic Seaport.

John is public program coordinator for Massachusetts Audubon's South Shore Sanctuaries. He lives in Weymouth, Massachusetts, with his wife, Michelle.

W. Russell Webster retired from the U.S. Coast Guard in 2003 after serving twenty-six years military service. While in the Coast Guard, Webster was Group Woods Hole rescue commander from 1998 to 2001 and led his service's operational response to the John F. Kennedy Jr. and Egypt Air 990 crashes. He was also the Coast Guard's regional operations officer for the September 11 terrorist attack responses.

Captain Webster is a maritime historian who specializes in Cape Cod–area rescues. His current projects include the search for RCS *Bear* and CGC *Escanaba* and an update on the *Sol e Mar* tragedy that changed Coast Guard procedures addressing apparent hoax calls.

He is a graduate of the U.S. Coast Guard Academy, Naval Postgraduate Schools in Newport, Rhode Island, and Monterey, California, and holds an MS in Systems Technology and an MA in National Strategic Studies. Webster is a senior official with the Transportation Security Agency at Logan International Airport in Boston. He resides in Cape Elizabeth, Maine, with his wife, Elizabeth, and two children, Andrew and Noelle.